In Good Company

In Good Company

The essential business start-up guide for women

Rebecca Jordan and Kirsty Weir

A & C Black • London

First published in Great Britain 2006

A & C Black Publishers Ltd
38 Soho Square, London W1D 3HB

© Clear Content Ltd, 2006

British Library Cataloguing in Publication Data
A CIP record for this book is available from the British Library.

ISBN-10: 0–7136–7626–4
ISBN-13: 978–0–7136–7626–6

A & C Black uses paper produced with elemental chlorine-free pulp, harvested from managed sustainable forests.

Design by Fiona Pike, Pike Design, Winchester
Typeset by RefineCatch Limited, Bungay, Suffolk
Printed in the United Kingdom by Bookmarque, Croydon

Contents

Thanks

We would like to say a big thank you to the following: our families and our wonderful husbands for all their support, Dave for his contacts, to all the brilliant businesses who have contributed to this book and to those good angels, business and otherwise, who have helped us along the way.

Introduction

THROUGHOUT THIS BOOK you will learn a lot about how we set up and grew our business over a five-year period. The business is still growing and changing. We started with an idea for a youth travel website at Gapwork.com. This then became a publishing company, and then we started to sell into schools and build the range. We are now an educational publishing company, employing a team of people, and selling into over 70% of the UK schools market. This year we have re-branded Gapwork Ltd as PDC Education Ltd, to reflect better the fact that it has become an educational publisher. It may seem at times that there has been little strategic planning involved in the course of our business, but while strategic planning is important, far *more* important for the survival and growth of a start-up business is being able to adapt to change and to capitalise on new opportunities. This is what makes running your own business exciting – the fact that things change all the time and that new opportunities rear their heads on a regular basis.

When we started out, we had no idea of what we personally were capable of achieving. But change forces you to take action and, before we knew it, we were employing a team of people, managing production processes, speaking at large events, pitching to major blue-chip companies and meeting Gordon Brown!

One of the best things about deciding to set up your own business is knowing that you will never be bored. You will never clock-watch. You will never wonder how you can kill time until 5.30 pm. You will never know what is around the corner. If this sounds like a challenge, it is. Read on and decide if you are up for it!

THE 'ENTREPRENEUR' THING

When we set up our business, we never had a grand vision of how it would grow or develop. We started out with an idea for a website, which we got up and running, and then just kind of went with the flow – using our skills the best we could, learning fast and not being afraid to venture into the unknown. Over a five-year period, the website idea developed into an educational publishers, employing 15 people, producing up to four new products a year and turning over three-quarters of a million pounds.

When we were approached to write a book about our experiences, we wondered whether we were qualified to do so. After all, we weren't running a multi-million pound corporation. But then we realised that the sum of our experience was greater than the size of our company; we could certainly share some of this experience if it might help other people considering going it alone. We gained some public recognition when we won the Parcelforce & Sunday Express Young Entrepreneur of the Year award in 2003, and then went on to write business advice columns for the *Yorkshire Post* and the *Sunday Express* – so the idea of a whole book wasn't too far from what we were doing already.

It is an interesting concept, being an entrepreneur, and one which hadn't really occurred to us before going for the award. Entrepreneurs are people like Richard Branson or Philip Green – people who start with nothing and end up building huge businesses and being multi-millionaires. We wouldn't object to owning our own jets or giving ourselves £1.2 billion dividend payouts, but we never wanted to run a business which would mean spending all our time in the office or on the road and employing hundreds of people. The world of corporate dog-fighting was not what we had in mind when we wanted to set up our own business. In fact, we knew that we wanted to do something completely different to what the world of suits, career ladders, office politics and clock-watching had to offer. Our key priorities were to make enough money to live the lifestyle we wanted to live, to do something creative and interesting, and to work together, as we had been friends for a few years and thought that we could work well in partnership.

So did this make us entrepreneurs? Entrepreneurial skills include the ability to adapt well to change, to take calculated risks, to think creatively, to solve problems effectively and to have a 'can-do' attitude. This being the case, we definitely are entrepreneurial and we are proud to say so. Entrepreneurs have a somewhat one-dimensional representation in the UK media. Branson, Green and Stelios are held up frequently as the definitive entrepreneurs – the flipside being the slightly shady wheeler dealers, the Del-boy type. We would venture to say that there are few women running their own businesses in the UK who would identify with any of these men when it comes to considering themselves as entrepreneurs.

But there is more to being an entrepreneur than just making loads of money. The skills we have already mentioned –

creative thinking, adapting to change, risk-taking etc – are skills which anybody running their own business needs to develop, regardless of the size of that business. To run a successful business of any shape or size requires the owner/manager of that business to show some entrepreneurial skills. If your business is a success, then you are using your entrepreneurial skills; you are therefore an entrepreneur. It is time to reclaim the word 'entrepreneur' from the slightly dubious media territory which it occupies at the moment and use it in a positive way to describe what you have to be on a daily basis to make your business succeed. Describing yourself as an entrepreneur should be a positive, life-affirming statement. We hope that this book enables more women to describe themselves as entrepreneurs with confidence and self-belief.

THE 'SMALL BUSINESS' THING

Size isn't everything. It's a tough one for many people to get their heads around, but there are very many hugely successful businesses which are relatively small in terms of turnover, number of employees and profitability. 'But how can this be?' we hear a multitude of business writers, analysts and leaders exclaim. It is simply because the success of a business is, or should be, defined by the person who sets it up. As an owner/manager of a business, your success could be defined by many things unrelated to turnover or profitability. You could define it by the amount of time it allows you to spend with your family, by how good the relationship is that you have with your customers, or by the creative challenges it gives you. Obviously a business has to make money to survive, but this is only a means to the personal satisfaction of the individual running that business. The success of a business is to some extent a subjective thing. If the owner/manager is happy with what they do, then they judge the business to be a success. This personal relationship between an individual and the business they set up is difficult for the outside world to understand. Hence the reason that a business is usually described as 'successful' when it is making lots of money, as this is easy to identify and measure.

We know this isn't the case and we want to challenge the traditional 'size and growth' definition of business success in this book. Just because you don't want to be the next Richard Branson or Anita Roddick (see how we struggle to identify another female entrepreneur who everyone will have heard of) doesn't mean that you can't run a brilliantly successful business and proudly describe yourself as an entrepreneur.

So what you won't find in this book is a magic recipe for making a million. There are no get-rich-quick tips or advice from billionaires about how they went from corporate take-over to strategic merger to buy their Caribbean island. What you *will* find is lots of firsthand experience from other women who run businesses that are successful on their own terms.

THE 'WOMAN' THING

We have met many women running their own businesses in the last five years. These vary from small enterprises that pay their owners enough money to meet the bills and go on holiday twice a year, through to women running operations with multi-million pound turnovers and hundreds of employees. There is no shortage of women starting and running their own business, it's just that you don't often hear about them. So when we were talking about writing this book, we thought, well it's got to be a positive thing, because we know there are lots of women out there who are thinking about setting up their own business or who are already running one. We wanted to include input from women owner/managers, and we wanted to get advice from experts who happen to be female.

This isn't through any bra-burning ambition to exclude men entirely, however. It is simply a redressing of the balance in terms of business writing. Pick up any business supplement, any top-100 list on business topics, business magazine or website, and you could be forgiven for thinking that women don't work at all. There might be a handful of women mentioned, but this is disproportionate to the reality of the situation – which is that there are plenty of successful female entrepreneurs out there, they are just either reluctant to identify themselves as such, or they do not have access to the media in order to boost their profile.

The focus on women in this book isn't meant to exclude men from its readership. Many (if not most) of the issues faced by women starting up are common to businesses owned by men too. But by concentrating on women-owned businesses, we are hopefully helping the reader to identify with and be inspired by our own experiences and those of other women.

HOW THE BOOK WORKS

Each chapter is designed to be read either as part of the whole book, or in isolation. We know that when you are setting up your own business you don't have a lot of spare time for ploughing through books. So just pick it up when you are in need of some general information or inspiration, or when you want to know how we dealt with something specific.

The chapters are organised roughly in terms of the themes you will need to tackle when planning your business or when running it in the early days – first comes the idea, then the requirement for funding, then for staff and so on. At the end of each chapter there is a brief summary to recap on what has gone before.

Most chapters include case studies of women who have successfully set up their own businesses. These include websites, training organisations, day nurseries, manufacturers and lots more besides. We deliberately wanted a wide range of enterprises to be included, to illustrate our point that women are running businesses of all shapes and sizes. The chapters also contain sections called 'Get the Basics' which are simply summary sections covering the core issues.

You will notice that we don't cover tax and red tape in much depth. This is because it is difficult to offer really helpful information on these for all businesses without going into masses of detail. To find out more about these issues, go to the business support organisations in the 'Useful Links' section on page 238, where you can get answers straight from the horse's mouth. If you can't find the information you need online, try calling the relevant organisation direct. We have always found Companies House, the Inland Revenue and ACAS very helpful when it comes to getting information and guidance about company law administration, tax, VAT and employment law, for example.

We are conscious that in telling our story in a totally honest, 'no holds barred' fashion, we are telling it warts and all. We would hate for the warts to deter anyone from having a go at setting up something that they believe in. Our problems won't necessarily be your problems, and by reading about them, you will hopefully learn from our experience and be aware of the pitfalls. Running your own business should be one of the greatest challenges that you face. It could change your life and the lives of those around you, so it would be irresponsible of us not to highlight things that can go wrong, as well as the things that are great about it.

Have fun with what you do and accept that while you can't do everything, you can still have a bloody good go. The stakes are as high as you want to make them – and if your business is a success, you will be not only financially better off, but you will have achieved the work/life balance which you have always dreamed of.

1

The Idea

IF YOU WERE TO ASK A DOZEN PEOPLE what the key to business success is, the chances are that you would get a variety of answers. Some people would say that business success is all about money, because if you don't make enough of it, you won't stay in business for very long. Others would claim that it is all about people and that relating well to both staff and customers is the most essential factor.

For us, the key to business success is the idea. Obviously we agree that a successful business also needs to make money, and that it's important to recruit the right people and relate well to customers. But without a good idea to begin with, everything else is just window dressing.

THE RIGHT IDEA

Everything that you see around you was once someone's bright idea – from the electric lights in your office to your desk and even the book you are now holding in your hands. Although each of these things is very real right now, they all started as nothing more than an idea.

Contrary to popular belief, coming up with the right idea – one that other people will pay for or buy into – is not rocket science. In this chapter we will explain how ideas can be generated, how you can develop them and how you can protect them. We will also supplement this with a variety of case studies so that you can see how the various principles we share have been applied to great effect in the real world.

In 2005, Deborah Leary won the British Female Inventor of the Year Award for her work with her company, Forensic Pathways Ltd (FPL). This is her account of how it happened.

In March 2001, I had just left my post as a training and development manager in education and was due to commence a lecturing post at a college in Sutton Coldfield, teaching Business Administration. During the three-week break between the two jobs, I attended the Forensic Identification Conference in Toronto with my husband, who was speaking at the conference. He was at this time a serving police officer with West Midlands Police.

During the course of the conference, I became involved in a discussion between officers from different forces and countries, relating to the procedures and equipment used in each jurisdiction. One piece of equipment – the crime scene stepping plate – was found to be used in the UK only and was not known to the Canadian forces. (Stepping plates are low-level platforms that are placed on the floor of a crime scene so that an investigator can walk through it without causing cross contamination or the destruction of evidence.) I still have the original hotel notepaper on which I made a note to find out about the plates and to set up a company to supply to Canadian forces!

Back in the UK, I obtained a sample of the plates and found that, while useable, they were not necessarily fit for their purpose. They were aluminium, heavy, covered with ridges which could trap dirt, could not be stacked and, most importantly of all, were not transparent. With no knowledge of the plastics/moulding industry, I set about investigating the possibility of designing a plate which could revolutionise crime scene management, providing a transparent, lightweight, stackable product. The key to this was liaising with the end user, sending out a mailshot outlining the design of the new FPL plates. The response was outstanding, giving a clear indication that there was a market and that it was ready for change.

Visit FPL's site at: www.forensic-pathways.com

Many people get their business ideas through the kind of personal experience that comes from having an interest in a particular hobby or by working in a particular field as an employee. Others get their ideas by listening to other people's experiences. Our own idea stemmed from the observation that that there was no website on the Internet which gave young people the information they needed to find seasonal work abroad. Both of us had both worked overseas, in Australia and Italy respectively, so we had firsthand experience of how difficult it could be. We'll tell you more about how we fleshed out this spark of an idea a little later, but first we need to take a temporary detour in order to discuss . . .

THE RIGHT ATTITUDE

Although having a good idea is important, it isn't enough by itself. After all, there are thousands of people who have good ideas all the time and never do anything with them. The missing ingredient is confidence; it is this that enables you to take your ideas further, to act on them. If an idea on its own is a good one, then when it is coupled with a confident attitude it can be an incredibly powerful thing.

Being entrepreneurial means being optimistic and believing that anything is possible. This doesn't come easily to many people, but it is a skill that can be developed if you go about it the right way. This means disciplining yourself to think more positively whenever you are presented with opportunities and taking control over the voice in your head. Many people, when they come across an opportunity, immediately hear a gloomy inner voice which provides a long list of reasons why they aren't in a position to jump at the chance. This kind of negative self-talk is largely habitual and is completely unrelated to what you are really capable of, so you should get into the habit of transforming all your pessimistic thoughts into their optimistic opposites, as below:

★ Whenever you catch yourself saying 'I can't', say 'I can!'
★ Whenever you want to say 'no' just because you think you might fail, say 'yes!'
★ Whenever you start listing all of the reasons why you can't do something, ask yourself the question 'How can I make this work?' instead.

It is amazing how changing the way that you think, about yourself and the opportunities that come your way, can have an immediate positive impact on your life. You don't have to stand in front of the mirror and affirm belief in yourself at every opportunity (although this works for some), but by developing the simple habit of thinking more positively, you will experience a subtle change in the way that you perceive the world.

As we said a moment ago, thinking in this way doesn't come easily to many people. Being a bit cynical, pessimistic and self-deprecating is something peculiarly British, and maybe women are more self-deprecating than men. But to get your business idea really up and running, you need to believe in it. You also need to be able to persuade other people to believe in it too. The only way that you can do all of this is by being relentlessly positive and open-minded, and by telling other people why your idea is such a fantastic one. If they can't or won't feel the same way about your idea, then that's their problem. Keep on going and you will find that there are always plenty of other people out there who will share your vision if you project it with enthusiasm.

This positive outlook on life is often described as a 'can-do attitude'. To those of us with small children, the phrase immediately conjures up an image of flushable toilet tissue – but it is probably the best way of describing the mental approach you need to have to get where you want to be in life.

IDENTIFYING THE BEST IDEA

Ideas, like buses, rarely turn up in isolation. Instead you will find that ideas have the habit of following hot on the heels of one another. In other words, once you have had one good idea, you can often expect another to pop up, and then another, and yet another. This could leave you facing the welcome challenge of having to decide which of your ideas is the best one to pursue.

Choosing between ideas effectively is something that can only be done by asking yourself a number of specific questions and taking the time to answer each of them to the best of your ability. In our experience, the four key questions you need to ask are as follows:

1 How much money could the idea make?

You will obviously have to take a bit of a guess at this stage, but if you focus on the potential market for the idea then you will have a fair clue as to how profitable it could be. For example, if your idea is to grow organic vegetables in your own garden, then you aren't likely to land a major contract with a national chain of supermarkets. However, if the idea is for a propagation gadget that would enable people to grow their own organic vegetables more effectively, the market for that idea – and therefore the potential profit – would be much bigger.

2 How would the implementation of the idea affect your life?

Turning an idea into reality is not something that happens automatically. It requires effort, energy, time and money. However, some ideas are likely to be more demanding than others. So you need to take a good look at your existing commitments and examine honestly what impact the idea would have on your life if you were to take action on it. If the price for going ahead is too high, you either need to change your existing commitments or to favour a different, less demanding idea.

3 How much value potential does the idea have?

We're not talking about value in terms of potential profit here, because we've already assessed that. Rather, we are talking about the value that the idea could bring to the lives of other people. It is always more fulfilling to take action on an idea that will serve others as well as ourselves. This kind of idea is also much more likely to be successful. As the American motivational speaker Zig Ziglar often says, 'You can have anything in the world you want if you'll just help enough other people get what they want.'

4 Would the pursuit of the idea make the most of your skills?

We all have a wide range of skills developed over the course of our lives, whether through our hobbies and interests or our work experience. If you can use your existing skills, then you won't need to spend time and energy learning new ones. You will also have a better chance of succeeding. So it makes sense to give preference to those ideas and business models that make the most of the skills and abilities that you already have in place.

All entrepreneurs find it hard to say 'no' to a good idea, so don't get hung up if you feel reluctant to put one or more on the back-burner in order to concentrate on those most likely to succeed. We are only human and we can therefore only do so much. The more balls you try to juggle at any given time, the more likely you are to drop one, so pursue only your best ideas and leave the others for later. They will always be there should you have more time to devote to them in the future.

THE RIGHT TIME

You can have a great idea and a positive attitude, but without the circumstances being right, it will remain an idea rather than becoming a business. 'Circumstances' include your personal situation, the state of the market, the economic climate and lots of other things that you can't do much about.

REBECCA SAYS:

When I came up with the idea for a website which eventually became Gapwork.com, I was 27 years old and had just finished an expensive and time-consuming Master's degree in law. The original idea had been for me finally to get a 'proper job' as a solicitor. However, events took a turn for the unexpected when, in my final year, I found out that I was pregnant. I couldn't face the idea of having a new baby and doing my training contract as a solicitor. My daughter was about a year old when Kirsty came back from Australia and we talked seriously about setting up the website. While it was difficult at first, balancing time with my daughter and time with the business, I was ready for a new challenge. The circumstances were right.

KIRSTY SAYS:

I had gone from university to running my own business, but when my business partner decided to follow her dream and become an actress, I found myself working for various marketing agencies. All the while I was looking at my bosses and thinking that I could run a business better than them! Eventually I took a career break and spent six months in Australia, working on a horse farm. When I came back to England, I carried on working with horses – but I knew I'd have to get a more highly paid job at some point. When Becca spoke to me about the website I could see the potential and thought, why not? I didn't have anything to lose at that point.

Whenever we speak about the development of ideas for businesses, many people ask us to share our own experiences.

So here's a little about how we have both come up with successful ideas in the past.

It was 1999 and I received a phone call from an old friend who wanted to find out more about working abroad. All he wanted to do was work in a bar in France over the summer. He was an experienced bar manager, so he had all the necessary skills that would be required.

The problem was that he couldn't find any suitable jobs advertised anywhere. He didn't want to take a massive risk and simply go to France and start looking for work. Instead he wanted to do things the sensible way by making some initial contacts, sending them his CV and trying to get something lined up in advance, even if was just a few promising interviews. He rang me in desperation because he knew that I had worked in Italy for a while. When I checked out the job situation, I was amazed to find that there really weren't any websites that helped young people find seasonal work abroad.

It occurred to me that this would be a really simple project to set up; employers would post advertisements and jobseekers would respond to these by e-mail or phone. Kirsty had recently returned from a career break in Australia and, having already run a business and worked in marketing, she was used to spotting a good opportunity. She thought that the market in Australia was a growing one and that we should start by focusing on that. So we did, and that's how Gapwork got started.

HOW THE IDEA FOR KIRSTY'S PREVIOUS BUSINESS CAME ABOUT

KIRSTY SAYS:

We were all into clubbing in our student days. The dance music scene in the mid-90s was massive, and all the big clubs had equally massive queues outside them every weekend. A friend of ours mentioned something about handing out flyers to people in the queues, and my friend Louisa and I thought about how we could develop this into handing out a pocket-sized magazine or goody bag which clubbers would want to take home with them. The idea was that corporate business would be keen to advertise with us and reach this audience.

Louisa and I went on to be Shell Livewire finalists with this very idea and soon had sponsorship from corporate companies including Sony, Carlsberg-Tetley, Boots and Durex.

JENNY UNGLESS RUNS CITY LIFE COACHING

City Life Coaching provides career advice to young professionals aged 20–30 who want to change their career paths to improve their prospects or adjust their work-life balance. Jenny started her business when she realised that she had reached a crossroads in her own career:

My background was in the Civil Service (six years) and politics (four years). I ended up as chief of staff to Iain Duncan Smith MP when he was leader of the Conservative Party. I left because I was tired of politics and felt that I was getting stale after so long in one area. I didn't know what I wanted to do next – I only knew what I didn't want to do! I found it difficult to find support in searching for a new career direction, apart from what was available in books. I felt that I couldn't be the only person in my 30s who was struggling with this issue, so I thought there might be an opportunity to provide career coaching to other young professionals. It became clear when I researched the market that setting up my own business was the obvious route to take, as there were few – if any – companies offering this kind of service.

**Visit City Life Coaching's site at:
www.citylifecoaching.com**

In all of these cases, the businesses were started either because of a perceived need or because of a well-spotted opportunity. Another important factor in each was that the timing was right, both in terms of the market and the life stages of the individuals involved. Other reasons for starting a business could include the desire to do something better than an existing company, or simply to do something that you love and enjoy.

Wherever the idea comes from, it is acting on it that really counts – and you can only do that effectively if the timing is right. Very often a business idea is triggered into action by personal circumstances. This could be the birth of a child, a redundancy, a divorce, or even the loss of a loved one. All of these events can make you reassess your lifestyle and your work choices in a significant way.

Louise Goulding set up her own business when she lost a member of her family in tragic circumstances. She says:

When my cousin Cassie was murdered at the age of 18 in 2003, a friend of the family built a website in her memory, which you can see at **www.cassiebrown.org**. The site was such a support to my friends and family that I wanted to share the idea. So **www.sharemymemory.com** was born.

When Cassie died, I was a marketing manager at O2 (formerly BT Cellnet). The salary and perks were great but I was miserable, an unfulfilled corporate slave, working a 60–80 hour week and commuting between Hammersmith, Slough and Leeds (I live in Sheffield). I'd always dreamed of setting up my own business, but I was waiting for my big idea, which came along in the most unexpected way.

Cassie and I had talked about setting up a company together. With her death, I realised that this was my chance to make a difference in her name and to help other people who had also been bereaved. When I explored the idea, through desk-based research (to size the market and check out the competition) and by talking to funeral directors, I realised that the idea of creating memorial websites was a really viable business proposition. Making it a reality was a challenge, as the concept met with bafflement (and sometimes derision) from funding bodies and banks alike. However, I negotiated a redundancy settlement from my job, got funding from Business Link and got cracking. My website went live in February 2004. Since then the business has expanded to provide baby and wedding websites in addition to the original memorial websites, but the idea is the same – to celebrate life's special people and events.

DO YOU HAVE TO LOVE YOUR IDEA?

Many people have said to us that we must be passionate about the idea of a gap year to start a business around it. Interestingly, we aren't. We both have a drive to make a business idea work, but we aren't precious about the idea itself. When the gap year website reached its natural plateau, we had already developed new products for new markets. While being passionate about something obviously helps to get it off the ground, becoming too fixed on one idea and not being able to see beyond it can actually limit your success.

FINDING YOUR INSPIRATION

So we've talked about finding the right idea at the right time and having the right attitude. We've mentioned ideas that are triggered by an identified gap in the market, or an opportunity that is too good to miss. But how else might you come up with an idea for a business? There are many people out there who would love to set up their own business and work for themselves, but how can they if they haven't had that 'Eureka!' moment? If you have a driving passion or a hobby which you'd be happy to do full-time, then you just need to work out how you can make money out of it. But what if you only know that you want to be your own boss?

The problem is that very often there doesn't seem to be time to get inspired. Would Newton have discovered gravity if he'd been rushing past that apple tree to pick up the kids? Would Bill Gates be where he is today if he'd had to do a big shop at Tesco? And there are so many distractions – television, radio, mobile phones, home computers, the Internet, sorting the car, sorting the house, snatching time with friends in between work and home – it's no wonder that people struggle to discover what they really want to do with their working lives.

On the other hand, ideas don't come in isolation. You need to have triggers, inspiration. It is by talking to people, meeting new people and listening that you find out about people's needs. This can be the thing that leads to your business idea.

TOP TIPS FOR FINDING INSPIRATION

1 Write down all of the things that you enjoy doing, then think about the business possibilities that could be associated with them. For example, if you like organising and managing things, you might consider starting a business as a freelance personal assistant or a wedding planner. Similarly, if you like horse riding you could explore setting up a riding school or selling equestrian accessories to stables.

2 Take some time out from your daily routine to look into new avenues. Browse online websites, pick up books and magazines that you wouldn't normally read or tune in to a radio or television station which is new to you. There may not be any obvious points of interest at first, but you just might hear, see or read something that sparks a good idea.

3 Take your interests one step further by taking classes or training. This will help you decide if your hobby is something you would like to do as a career. For example, if you have enjoyed aerobics for a few years, you could consider training to become an aerobics instructor or personal trainer.

4 Think about things that are important to you personally. Are you passionate about human rights? Do you have strong views on the environment and conservation? Very often, the chance to do something more meaningful on a daily basis can compensate for a drop in salary or benefits. Try volunteering your services first with a charity to see if you can deal with working at the sharp end.

🖥 Find a partner. The prospect of setting up a business on your own can be daunting. Try talking to friends and find out if anyone else is thinking of setting up on their own. There are loads of businesses that have been set up on the basis of successful partnerships, and having each other as mutual support can be a life-saver.

GET THE BASICS: YOU DON'T ALWAYS NEED YOUR OWN IDEA

While having your own unique and original idea for a new business is never a bad thing, it isn't absolutely essential. There are various other ways in which you can achieve great success using the good ideas of other people. Not by stealing them, of course, but by taking one of the perfectly legal and ethical approaches detailed here. . .

Buy a franchise

Franchising is an arrangement where the owner of a proven business format (known as the franchisor) sells other people (the franchisees) a licence to run the same business in a specific area (known as the territory). For example, every branch of McDonalds or KFC that you visit is a franchise, where the manager has paid a fee for the right to run that business in that location.

The benefits of buying a franchise are numerous. First, you know in advance that the business model works, because you can see it working elsewhere. Second, all of the planning is done for you, as each franchise comes with its own line of products or services, its own operating and staff procedures, and its own advertising materials. And last, but not least, franchising enables you to get into business for yourself but not by yourself, as most franchisors offer full training and ongoing support.

There are thousands of different franchise opportunities on the market, offering you the chance to sell everything from fitted kitchens to garden landscaping to fast food. While some franchises are expensive (as in six figures), there are also many that can be started for a lot less – sometimes for as little as a couple of thousand pounds. Because of the sheer range of opportunities on offer, you should be careful to research the available franchises thoroughly; getting involved is a big decision and not something to rush into. We recommend that your first port of call should be the British Franchise Association (**www.british-franchise.org**) who offer advice, information and inexpensive seminars on all aspects of franchising.

Buy a going concern

A going concern is a business which is already up and running, but which is now for sale because the owner wants to move on to something else. Take a look through newspapers such as *Dalton's Weekly* and you will see a variety of going concerns for sale all over the country, from ice cream parlours in Brighton to newsagents in London to fish and chip shops in Sheffield.

The biggest advantage of buying a going concern is that all the hard work of setting up and getting established has already been done for you. With a regular client base in place, all you have to do is step into the present owner's shoes and keep things running smoothly.

Of course, you do need to exercise caution when buying a

going concern, because not all businesses are actually as profitable as their owners say they are. Look at all leases, accounts and licences carefully, rather than automatically assuming that the owner is telling the truth, and always make sure that any deal is made through a qualified and experienced solicitor. With these caveats in mind, buying a going concern is often a great way to get into business quickly and without all the fuss of starting from scratch.

Buy into an existing business
A third option for those who don't want to pursue an original idea is to buy into an existing business. Sometimes a successful, well-established business will want to expand, either by taking on a partner or by setting up a separate branch in a second location. This can generate opportunities for you to buy a share of the business and get involved in the expansion.

Other businesses occasionally look for 'sleeping partners' – individuals who are willing to invest in the business in return for a proportional share of the profits, but who aren't particularly interested in getting involved in a 'hands on' way.

Both approaches can work well, as long as you always remember the motto 'buyer beware' and investigate the business thoroughly before putting any money down. And of course, arranging any deal through a solicitor is essential.

As you can see, there's no reason why not having an original business idea should stop you from becoming a successful businesswoman. The three approaches outlined here enable anyone with the necessary self-belief and capital to take their dream and make it a reality, so you would do well to give them all your serious consideration.

FINDING OUT ABOUT YOUR COMPETITION

Sometimes you need to find out more about what competitors are up to. While we wouldn't advise donning a balaclava and attempting corporate espionage, there are perfectly legal and above-board ways of having a snoop.

★ Go to **www.companieshouse.gov.uk** and pay a small fee to read published accounts. You can find out who the directors of relevant companies are, how many shares they own and how much money each business makes. This could have a real impact on your business decisions. If they aren't making any money, you could decide that your model isn't different enough from theirs and you will be unlikely to make money with your idea either. Alternatively, they could be making millions because they have total dominance in a market and you will need to radically rethink your approach to steal a march on them.

★ You can ring up competitors and talk to them without telling them too much about who you are or what you do. Obviously they aren't about to tell you anything confidential, but if you are smart you can find out key names in the organisation, what their job titles are, and the size of the company.

★ Do your desk research. Use the Internet to find articles and information about competing companies by searching on **www.google.com**. Dig around on the company websites and you can find lots of useful information about their existing products and services, new ones they may be launching and their customers.

★ Speak to their customers. Find out who uses their products and get feedback from them about the quality of the product or service. You will also get a feel for whether your alternative version will be well received.

The point of doing all this is that it will reinforce your idea – or it may undermine it. Either way, you need to understand how your idea will fit within the present market place and how it stands alongside competitors.

GET THE BASICS: PROTECTING YOUR INTELLECTUAL PROPERTY

Intellectual property is generally defined as any idea or expression of an idea that has potential commercial value. For example, a unique recipe for a new kind of chocolate-chip cookie could be considered intellectual property. And so could any particularly catchy name you come up with for your business.

Because good ideas such as these are the lifeblood of any successful business, it is important that you consider protecting your intellectual property so that it isn't stolen or otherwise hijacked by your competitors. There are several ways of doing this and you should familiarise yourself with all of them at the outset:

Patents

A patent is used to protect a product or a process of product creation which features a brand-new invented element. So if you have invented a new and unique board game for kids, or a new way to manufacture washing up liquid, you can probably patent it in order to keep your invention safe.

Patents are issued by the government and, once granted, make the holder the legal owner of the invention. However, it is important to note that patents are only valid in the territory in which they are issued. A patent issued in the UK would therefore protect your rights in the UK, but not necessarily in other countries.

While there are a number of companies that will, for a fee, help you protect your inventions using the patent process, applying for a patent directly from the UK Patent Office isn't complicated and will almost always be the more economical option. For further details, visit the Patent Office's website at **www.patent.gov.uk** or call its Central Enquiry Unit on 0845 9 500 505.

Trademarks

A trademark is a unique mark that is used to identify a specific product or business. Examples can include:

★ **Logos, such as the British bulldog of the Churchill insurance company, or the red telephone of Direct Line.**
★ **Images, like the portrayal of Mickey Mouse or Bart Simpson.**
★ **Product names, such as Coca Cola, Pepsi or Juicy Fruit.**
★ **Business and/or personal names, as in IBM, Virgin, Disney and McDonalds.**

While there is no law that says you absolutely must register a trademark, registering enables you to take swift legal action against any company using a similar trademark in the future to promote a similar product or service. This helps to ensure that your trademark remains unique to you and protects you from potentially devastating situations, such as other companies counterfeiting the trademark and passing off their own products as yours.

Trademark registration in the UK is achieved through the Patent Office, so once again you can visit the website at **www.patent.gov.uk** or call 0845 9 500 505.

Non-disclosure agreements

Sometimes it is necessary to share confidential information about your business with a third party in order to take the business forward. For example, you may hire a copywriter to write advertisements for a new product you've come up with and he or she may need quite a lot of detail about this product in order to do his or her job properly.

In cases such as these you should use non-disclosure agreements (also known as NDAs or confidentiality agreements) to protect the information you share.

The NDA is a fairly simple but legally binding contract which prevents the third party (for example, the copywriter) from disclosing any of the confidential information you share with them. The contract is legally binding as soon as the third party signs it.

For more information on creating and using non-disclosure agreements, visit the Business Link website at **www. businesslink.gov.uk** and do a search on 'NDA'.

Copyright

Some ideas cannot be protected because they are too vague. For example, if you have an idea for a new movie which goes something like, 'a man pretends to be a woman in order to get the job of his dreams', then you can't protect that idea. However, the unique and fixed expression of such an idea can be protected with copyright. So if you actually wrote a screenplay that was based on the idea just mentioned (as *Tootsie* was), then the law of copyright would protect that screenplay.

Whereas patents and trademarks are registered rights (because there's a central register of patents and trademarks that have been issued), copyright is unregistered. This means that there are no formal procedures to go through and that copyright exists from the moment the material is set down on paper (or magnetic media). However, it is common for copyright to be expressly indicated by the standard copyright sign ©, followed by the year in which the copyrighted material was originally created.

PROTECTING YOUR IDEA

When we first came up with the idea for a website to help young people find out about working and travelling abroad, we spent some time agonising over whether it was better to talk to people about our idea and run the risk of someone stealing it, or to keep it to ourselves and run the risk of not getting enough advice about it. In our experience, it all depends on who you are thinking of talking to. Being completely open about your brilliant idea with a direct and established competitor would not be advisable. Even if they didn't copy you, they then have the advantage over you and could start defending their own products or services against your proposed idea.

But sometimes you need to talk to experts in the field who aren't necessarily your competitors. We tend to be quite open about our ideas and work on the theory that if someone else can be bothered to rip us off and get their product to market before us, then good luck to them. But this attitude is the result of five years of confidence building and ideas forming. We know that we don't have many direct competitors who can do stuff as quickly as we can. If you have one truly innovative idea, then there are ways in which you can protect it. So by all means use trademarks, patents or NDAs wherever you think applicable, but try not to be too precious about your idea. You need to share it with people for it to gather momentum, and you never know who might be listening – it could be a potential investor or an invaluable non-executive director in the making.

Who should you talk to about your idea?

★ Your family. Members of your family share their lives with you, so they need to understand what it is you are trying to do and any implications it will have for them.

★ Friends . . . as long as you trust their opinion. They might give you some insight into what they think your personal strengths and weaknesses are.

★ People who have succeeded in their own field. These people can give good general advice about what it is like to run your own business.

★ People who are doing what you want to do but who are further down the line. These people can offer brilliant specific advice and even support, if you are lucky. However, be careful about telling them too much about something which they could easily do themselves.

★ The Department of Trade and Industry, HM Revenue & Customs and any other government bodies that are relevant to what it is you are trying to do.

★ Accountants and lawyers. They will often give the first half hour of their time for free, so make the most of it.

The meeting will be confidential and you can get some
good pointers about where to take your idea next.

★ Banks, business angels, venture capitalists and financial
advisors. These are the kind of 'money people' that you
need to help you turn your idea into a successful reality.

★ Business Link and other business support agencies. It is
in the best interests of the country as a whole to have
new businesses start up and succeed, and because of this
there is a vast amount of information available that can
help you to get started.

The main thing to bear in mind when you are listening and
talking to these people is that all their advice, no matter how
impartial, will be subjective. In other words, it's based on their
own personal opinions. This being the case, you shouldn't
treat every word of advice you receive as if it were objective
fact. Our advice would be to take on board what you think is
relevant and act upon it where necessary; keep all the contacts
on good terms (you never know when they might come in
handy) but – when the rubber hits the road – follow your
instincts and use your common sense.

No matter how high up the person may be giving you
advice, they probably won't know as much about your business as you do, so don't hang on their every word. On the
other hand, if you know nothing and you are talking to someone who's been around for years, learn from them. Willingness
to learn and adapt are key survival techniques for entrepreneurs. That doesn't just mean adapting yourself either – it
means adapting your business idea. You can't afford to be
precious about it.

HAVING A PLAN B

The very first idea that we had for Gapwork.com was for a website that people would subscribe to in order to get up-to-date job vacancy details sent to them via e-mail while they were travelling. Remember that this was in the late 90s, when it seemed possible that people would actually pay to use websites. We did pretty well considering and we got around 30 people to subscribe, but we soon realised a key point. It wasn't going to make a lot of money. And it was hard work – it was labour intensive for little reward. As business models go, it wasn't up there with Google or eBay.

So what did we do? Did we cling onto our business model and try to make it work despite all evidence to the contrary? Did we give up on it altogether and go back to the day jobs? No, we went to Plan B.

To be perfectly honest our Plan B hadn't been around for long, but it was there at the time that we needed it. Our main issue was that, as a small business, we were unable to target the masses of young people out there who might want to travel abroad. Plan B came about by thinking of how we could sell a solid product to young people without having to have a multi-million pound marketing budget. Our website had loads of content on it, so we created a book: *The Australia and New Zealand Gap Pack*. We then realised that there was a demand for this kind of book in schools, so we started to build a database of secondary schools in the UK and sell it to them. Plan B seemed to be working. The idea of the subscription website was soon superseded by a different business model which was much more manageable for us.

Having a Plan B is essential for any new business. You need to be thinking constantly about other people you could sell to, new markets, new products, new services, new channels to market, the whole caboodle. Keep writing your ideas down, no matter how far-fetched they may seem, as you never know when you might need them.

Research and networking are key to the development of Plan Bs. You may meet someone at a networking event who offers a whole new market for your product or service which you had never thought of until then. Don't presume that you know all there is to know about what you are doing – external people can have a completely different take on things which can boost your business or shape your ideas enormously. When you are researching your idea, try to keep your reading and discussions as wide and as far-reaching as possible. Draw a huge spider chart with your business at the centre, and all the possible channels and markets coming out of it. Even if you are sure that there is no demand for what you do in say China, or Australia, don't discount it. Write it down – it could actually form part of your Plan B.

A brilliant example of someone having a winning Plan B is Spencer Silver, the inventor of the Post It note, who is mentioned in the following section.

TEN OF THE BEST BUSINESS IDEAS – EVER!

POST-IT. In 1964, Spencer Silver, a 3M chemist, set out to find an adhesive that was stronger than any other. He ended up finding an adhesive that stuck things temporarily, but never permanently. While other companies would have seen this as failure, 3M used the 'non-stick' adhesive to create Post It notes, which can now be found in offices and homes everywhere.

GOOGLE. In September 1998, former Stanford University students Larry Page and Sergey Brin had the idea of creating a new and better Internet search engine. Google is now one of the biggest media companies in the world.

AMAZON. In 1994, Jeff Bezos founded Amazon.com and launched what was to become the leading online book retailer. His vision of low prices, a vast selection and plenty of product information has been a winner all the way.

FORD. Henry Ford is best known for his cars (he founded the Ford Motor Company in 1903). But his real innovation was in the way in which he produced those cars. Ford invented assembly-line mass production – a manufacturing model now used to great effect in almost all sectors of business.

WOOLWORTHS. Frank and Charles Woolworth merged six chains of five-and-ten-cent retail stores in the US in 1911. Their vision was to 'pile it high and sell it cheap'. The idea worked on a massive scale and Woolworths is now one of the most famous retail chains in the world.

DYSON. James Dyson invented the world's first bagless vacuum cleaner in 1993. After many rejections and over 5,000 prototypes, the DC07 became the fastest selling vacuum cleaner ever to be made in the UK. Incidentally, there is some excellent information on patents and protecting your idea at **www.dyson.co.uk**.

ESTÉE LAUDER. In 1946, Estée Lauder filled a jam jar with a skin cream developed by her uncle (who was a chemist) and created her first product for sale. From those humble beginnings the Estée Lauder company has become one of the biggest cosmetics and fragrance companies on the face of the earth, with the brand being recognised in over 100 countries worldwide.

BODY SHOP. Driven by financial necessity, and with fair trade and environmental awareness at the core of her identity, Anita Roddick opened the first Body Shop store in 1976. Today there are 1,980 stores serving customers across the planet and Anita Roddick herself (now Dame Anita Roddick) has become a model of how it is possible to succeed in business and help the world at the same time.

MARY KAY COSMETICS. Mary Kay Ash worked as a sales director for a number of years before beginning to write a book on business. As the book developed, she realised that she was in fact creating a business plan. Together with her son, she started Mary Kay Cosmetics in 1963 as a way of putting that business plan into action. By the time she died in 1996, over 150 of her female cosmetics representatives had earned $1 million or more.

MARTHA STEWART LIVING. Martha Stewart worked as a successful stockbroker on Wall Street and it is there that she developed her early business acumen. In 1972, she started a catering business specialising in visually attractive recipes, some of which she later included in her first book entitled *Entertaining*. This was just the start of her business empire; her books, television shows, magazines and branded products have helped millions to create, maintain and enjoy their ideal homes and lifestyles. Her strong brand has survived even though Martha Stewart herself was sentenced to a spell in prison.

CENTRIFUGAL CHILDBIRTH. This novel idea, patented in 1965 by George Blonsky, was for 'Apparatus for Facilitating the Birth of a Child by Centrifugal Force'. The thinking was that the invention would utilise centrifugal force to assist the birth of a child, causing less stress to the mother.

WALKING ON WATER. The 'Device for Walking Upon the Surface of the Water' was patented in 1918 by Martin Jelaian, and employed a gas balloon so that the user could 'slidably [sic] walk through the water'.

COMBINED TORCH AND BATTLE AX. Patented by Abraham Wolf in 1884, the idea here was to 'provide combined torches and battle axes designed especially for use in torch light processions, and which shall be neat and ornamental in appearance.'

POGO SHOES. Patented in 1976, these were boots perched on a pogo stick with a wheel at the end. Think of riding one-wheeled roller skates on stilts. Maybe Death Traps would have been a better name.

ANIMAL TRACK SHOES. This idea from P. E. McMorrow was patented in 1968 and was for a pair of shoes which, thanks to the unique moulding of the soles, left animal tracks instead of footprints.

LOO GAMES. In 1988, Louis Douglas patented an 'Amusement Device for a Toilet Bowl or Urinal'. The invention featured urine sensors, buzzer sounds, LED lights and boasted the capacity to be 'connected to a video screen or a speaker disposed above the urinal for providing additional audial [sic] and visual stimulation to the user.'

BUDGIE NAPPIES. Yes, we know they can be messy, but do birds really need to wear nappies? This 1956 patent suggests that someone thought it was a good idea.

GRAVE ATTACHMENT. In 1908, G. H. Willems patented a 'Grave Attachment' which was basically a periscope-type device running from the foot of a coffin to the ground above – presumably so that grave visitors could see the corpse, and vice versa.

TOY DOG VACUUM CLEANER. A genuine patent from 1973 featured a life-size toy dog containing a vacuum cleaner. Handily, the vacuum could also be reversed as a blower 'to serve as a dryer'. Too bad the hose emerged from the dog's butt.

RUBBER TUNES. A 1992 patent outlined plans for a 'Force Sensitive, Sound Playing Condom'. And you thought romance was dead . . .

YOUR ELEVATOR PITCH

When we first had the idea for the Gapwork website, we would try to describe it to people as a one-stop-shop web portal for 16–30 year olds who were interested in working and travelling abroad on a gap year or career break and needed to find a job. Needless to say, the listener would quickly assume a glazed expression and switch off half way through.

Not because the business idea was boring (we've heard a lot worse!), but because people automatically tend to doze off whenever anyone takes more than a minute or two to describe something new. This is where the elevator pitch comes in.

The idea of the elevator pitch is that it summarises your business idea so concisely that it paints a thumbnail sketch of the whole concept in as few strokes as possible. Imagine that you get into a lift. You have a business idea and next to you is a potential investor who has just pressed the button to go down to the ground floor. You have exactly 30 seconds to sell your idea to the investor. If you have your 'elevator pitch' all ready to go, you're in business. Or, at the very least, you're in with a shot of getting someone to listen to your business concept.

The best way of creating an elevator pitch is to spend time scripting it, just as you might script any other speech or sales pitch. Get a pad and pen and then begin writing what you want people to know about your business, bearing in mind the 30-second time limit. Start by introducing yourself (or your company), then summarise what you do and say what makes your offering so special. When you've finished, commit the script to memory and get into the habit of taking lifts instead of the stairs. Yes, even when it's busy. The more people who hear your elevator pitch when you deliver it, the better.

To give you some idea of what a complete elevator pitch sounds like, here's the one we developed for Gapwork:

> **We are a team of gap year specialists with a unique website and magazine which helps young people find out about working and travelling abroad.**

Okay, so it's not going to win any prizes for being great

literature, but that's not the point of the exercise. An elevator pitch has to brief and concise. And if it sparks off more questions than it answers, all well and good – that's what it's designed to do!

It's a good discipline to turn every idea you have into an elevator pitch. Not only will this help you share your ideas more effectively with the people who count, but it will also help you to crystallise your own thinking in the process.

THE POWER OF THE WRITTEN WORD

There is something enormously powerful about the written word and when it comes to setting goals, we consider the act of writing them down to be indispensable. Writing down your goals forces you to think seriously about what you want out of life; it brings you face to face with the truth that you can have almost anything you want, if you would simply make a firm decision to go out and get it.

We set our goals at the beginning of each year. We write them in accordance with the same guidelines that you will be given in a few moments. Then, when we're done, we put our goals in a safe place so that we can review them regularly. If at some point we want to add a new goal, we do so. Being flexible enough to amend, change or add to our goals list is important, because as we go through life our desires and ambitions often change.

REBECCA SAYS:

One January I wrote that I was driving a new car – one that was more suited to my new role as a successful entrepreneur than the ancient one I had at the time. The next month there was a cold spell and someone slid into the back of my old banger and wrote it off while it was parked outside the office. The insurance company paid up and I got myself a shiny new car. Okay, so it wasn't exactly as I had planned it, but I got what I had written!

The moral is to be careful what you write down – because writing it down makes it more likely to come true!

OUR GOAL-WRITING GUIDELINES

Whenever we write down our goals, be they business or personal ones, the process we use is always the same. We recommend that you use the same guidelines and see for yourself just how powerful the written word can be.

Aim high

When you set your goals, aim high. Don't worry about how a goal can be achieved at this stage. Just focus on what you want in your life. Mix both business and personal goals. Set goals for the kind of body you want, the kind of car you want to drive, the kind of house you want to live in and the kind of business that you want to run. If your goals seem beyond your reach at this point in time, that's okay. If your objectives were already accessible to you then you wouldn't be putting them on your goals list in the first place! So be brave. Be confident. And aim high.

Be specific and measurable

Goals aren't really goals unless they are both specific and measurable. 'I want to be rich!' is not a goal, but merely a wish. Every Lotto player in the country has the same wish and only one in 14 million gets to see that wish come true.

However, 'I want to have £500,000 in the bank!' is not a wish. It's a goal because it is specific (you have stated the amount of money you want) and it is measurable (you can look at your bank statement and see instantly whether or not the goal has been achieved).

Write in the present tense

It is important to write your goals down in the present tense, as if they have already happened. For example, instead of writing 'I want to have £500,000 in the bank!', you should write 'I have £500,000 in the bank!' In the same way, instead of writing 'I want to own a thriving personal development book store', you should write 'I own a thriving personal development book store'.

Why is writing in the present tense so important? Because the subconscious mind can't tell the difference between fantasy and reality; if it believes something that *doesn't* match up with the external conditions of your life, it will actually guide you towards taking the kind of actions that are required to make reality fit the belief.

The written word is a powerful tool, and you should start using it right away by setting yourself some inspiring goals. But don't stop there. Get into the habit of writing down all of your ideas as you get them. In fact, why not go out and buy a nice notebook specifically for all the ideas you're going to come up with over the next few weeks? Any one of them could bring you all the success you desire, so it makes sense to write them down before they fade from your memory. Another advantage of doing this is that it provides a record of ideas that you can revisit in the future.

GET AN IDEAS PROCESS
Collate your ideas

Depending on whether you prefer to keep your information on a computer screen or on paper, open a folder on your PC or get a nice shiny ring-binder and start to collect your ideas in one place. Every time you have an idea, no matter how vague or unrealistic it may seem at the time, write it down and store it in your folder. By doing this you will start building a bank of ideas. It is always best to stockpile information and be able to return to it later, rather than try to keep absolutely everything in your head.

This principle of recording your ideas can be applied to any kind of thinking – whether it be a subject for your new novel, a business you'd like to own or the kind of lifestyle you would like to have. You don't necessarily have to write just ideas down, but anything that occurs to you which may influence your decision about your business. For example, you might read something of particular interest on the Internet, or someone might say something that makes you look at yourself slightly differently. Copy it all down in your ideas folder, because it's all potentially useful information.

Foster the right attitude

Remember the 'can-do' thing? Bear in mind that without a positive attitude, the best idea in the world will remain just an idea. But with an attitude of confidence and self-belief, you will be able to surmount all the obstacles that stand between you and making that idea become a tangible reality.

When the time is right, return to your ideas

When you have decided that you are definitely going to leave your job, or that you are definitely pregnant and want to work for yourself, or that you are definitely going to ignore everyone's advice and go it alone, or that you've had a windfall which means you can do something with the cash, return to your ideas file and start to look at each one. Develop your own criteria around what you think will make a successful business. This will probably include financial viability, what effect it would have on your lifestyle, what training or support you will need and so on. It may be that you want to run your ideas past someone else at this stage, or you may want to keep them completely to yourself and make your own decision, but now is the time to focus on what you've got so far.

It may be that nothing in your ideas folder is feasible, or even desirable, in which case you will need to do some more brainstorming. Alternatively, you may have two or three things which are equally attractive and you can't make your mind up. In that case, apply your criteria strictly, think through the implications carefully, give some serious consideration to each one and see if you can prioritise them in order of preference. Take a look at the competition and start to work up your idea into something resembling a mini-business plan. When assessing business ideas, make sure that you bear the following in mind:

★ your elevator pitch
★ your Unique Selling Proposition – what makes this idea unique?
★ how you will make money
★ how much money you will make
★ what you can bring to the business
★ who your major competitors are
★ what your Plan B is

With this kind of clarity and focus, it will be a lot easier getting your business to the next stage, which is thinking about how you will find the money necessary to get it up and running.

2

Money

WHEN WE STARTED GAPWORK, NEITHER OF US HAD any money
that we could put into our business. Rebecca hadn't had a
proper job for years and Kirsty had just got back from a career
break in Australia. We were still in that weird post-graduation
phase of life when we hadn't really found our niche or completely managed to get out of the student lifestyle. We didn't
have mortgages, savings or cars – in fact we had hardly
anything that was worth more than £50.

Starting from this position had both positive and negative
consequences. On the positive side, it meant that we had nothing to lose by starting our own business. We didn't have high
paying jobs to give up, with pensions, benefits or any other
perks. On the negative side, it made our search for start-up
funding that much harder.

The lack of finance and the financial risks involved in setting up your own business are key reasons why most people
choose to remain as employees rather than striking out by
themselves. One of the first things you should ask yourself
when thinking about going it alone is, 'What am I prepared to
risk for this?'. Try running through the following questions as
a kind of mini risk assessment:

* How much money do I need to start the business?
* When do I need to have started it by?
* How much time will I need to dedicate to it?
* How much time can I afford to dedicate to it?
* Will I have to give up work?
* Can I work part time and work on the business in the time remaining?
* How much money have I got in savings?
* At what point do I have to have made sales before I run out of money?
* How might starting a business impact on my family?
* Can I cover the mortgage/bills/other outgoings without relying on the business succeeding in the short term?
* How much of my own money am I prepared to put into the business?
* Am I prepared to secure finance against my home or car?
* Have I thought through all the costs involved in setting up the business?
* Is my partner (if relevant) willing and able to pay the bills for a while if they have to?

There is actually no need to 'risk it all' for the sake of a business. Some people choose to do so and put their homes or life savings on the line, but you can limit your risk by following our suggestions below:

* Be cautious when deciding what kind of business you want to set up – some types of business require a lot less investment than others.

★ Don't ditch the day job without having set up some definite sales leads, savings or other identifiable forms of income to pay the bills. If you are desperate to get out of your job and spend more time on the business idea, think about trying to find alternative part-time work as an intermediary measure.

★ Look into every possible source of funding that doesn't involve getting into personal debt. Business Link, Chambers of Commerce and your local council can point you in the direction of grants for research or marketing.

★ Always get quotes from at least three suppliers when you are looking for business services or products. Try to strike a balance between quality and price.

★ Talk to suppliers about terms of payment. The later the better.

★ Measure everything you do in terms of how much it will cost in relation to what business benefits will come out of it. If, for example, there is a trade show in Singapore which you think you should attend, cost out every aspect of it. Try to identify the reasons why you would want to attend, then work out how much money you could potentially make by going. If you can't identify immediate business benefits (and cash) from the trip, then think again about going.

SOURCES OF FUNDING

We initially looked at venture capitalists as a source of funding. In retrospect this was not right for our business plan, but bear in mind that this was at the time of the dot-com boom. Back then, every man and his dog seemed to be able to pitch an idea for a website at venture capitalists, who would respond by throwing millions at them in the hope that some of it would make massive gains.

The irony was that, while we were talking to venture capitalists about hundreds of thousands of pounds, we still needed to get the website up and running. We didn't need much, so we borrowed £500 from Rebecca's father, which we then paid to a freelance web designer to build a six-page website. People often ask if we paid Rebecca's father back, and the answer is yes, we did!

ADVERTISING AND SPONSORSHIP

One of the reasons why Kirsty had got involved with Gap-work in the first place was because she saw the potential of the website to get advertising from companies eager to reach our users. As soon as we had the website designed and had some site visitors, we approached a few blue chip companies with sponsorship opportunities. After chasing a handful of leads, we got a phone call from Boots, who were about to launch a gap year travel insurance policy and were keen to reach young people with their advertising. The phone call was welcome, but they wanted to come and meet us in Leeds. This was a problem, as at that point we were working from an office at home. We wanted Boots to buy into our ideas but also to buy into us as a credible young business, so we borrowed fancy office space for the meeting from a business acquaintance in the city centre. It must have done the job, as Boots advertised with us for a year and gave us enough money to live on while we were on the hunt for investment.

If your business model allows for some advertising or sponsorship opportunities and you have customers who might be interested in hearing from related companies, then it might be worth looking at advertising as a potential revenue source. To do this effectively, you need to understand your market, have an existing customer base, put together some kind of media pack and do a crash course in media sales – simple!

Advertising can take many forms, including partnerships, affiliate schemes and sponsorship deals, so think laterally about companies you could work with and how it would benefit your business. Sometimes partnerships might not be based on a simple payment basis, but through such a partnership your business could benefit from extending its reach into the market.

A crucial part of deciding how to fund your enterprise is choosing what kind of legal entity your business is going to be. There are advantages and disadvantages to all the options and the best thing to do is to talk to an expert accountant, solicitor or Business Link advisor about what kind of business you should be setting up. Find out more for yourself by reading the guidance documents available at Companies House (**www.companieshouse.gov.uk**). In the meantime, take a look at our outline below.

GET THE BASICS: CHOOSING YOUR TRADING STATUS

You have three main options when choosing a trading status for your new business: you can operate as a sole trader, as a partnership, or as a private limited company. There are pros and cons in each case, so let's look at all three options in more detail.

Sole trader

Operating as a sole trader is the simplest of all routes into business. All you have to do from a legal standpoint is tell the Inland Revenue and Department of Social Security about your new business (so that they can send you the necessary income tax and National Insurance information) and open a business bank account. Once you have done this, you are free to start running your business as you please. The main advantage of operating as a sole trader is this fundamental simplicity, but other advantages include:

★ You are able to keep your own accounts for tax calculation purposes. Of course, an accountant is almost always a beneficial expense, but there is no obligation to use one if you don't want to.
★ You can change your trading status at a later date if necessary, as your circumstances change.

The biggest disadvantage to operating as a sole trader is that you and the business are one and the same entity as far as UK law is concerned. This means that if someone sues your business, or it becomes unable to meet its debts, you will be held personally liable.

Partnership

Running a business as a partnership is very similar to running as a sole trader, except there are two or more people involved as equal partners. Each partner is personally responsible for business liabilities. This means that if one partner absconds with the contents of the bank account, the remaining partner(s) will have to pay the bills out of her own pocket, even if this involves filing for bankruptcy. Obviously, this state of affairs makes your choice of partner(s) extremely important, and it is vital to work only with someone who you trust implicitly. With that major disadvantage covered, the advantages of partnerships are:

★ **Ease of set up.** As when operating as a sole trader, all you need to do is advise the Inland Revenue and DSS of your business activities and open a business bank account.

★ **Shared workload and responsibilities.** Running a business can be hard work and sharing the load with someone who has an equally vested interest in seeing it succeed can be very helpful.

★ **A wider range of skills and abilities.** Going into partnership with someone who has different strengths and areas of expertise can help the whole business succeed far faster than if you were to try to develop new skills yourself as you go along.

Limited company

Both sole traders and partners are, as we have seen, personally liable for any liabilities incurred by their business. A limited company, however, limits the liability of those involved, because a company is viewed in law as an entity in its own right. This is the main advantage of setting up a limited company. Others include:

★ **A more professional profile.** In some cases, potential clients, employees and suppliers may have more faith in Joanne Bloggs, Ltd than they would in Joanne Bloggs, sole trader. Being a limited company (of any size) automatically says that you are serious about your business and aren't likely to disappear overnight.

★ Greater ease of funding. Having a limited company may make it easier for you to raise finance in the future from bank loans, venture capitalists and business angels.

The main disadvantages of setting up and running a limited company are:

★ A limited company is slightly more complicated to set up and involves quite a bit of red tape and paperwork as you communicate with Companies House. This task can be made much easier by enlisting the help of an accountant or solicitor.

★ Limited companies are not allowed to submit their own accounts. Instead, all accounts must be audited by a professional accountant.

★ The laws concerning the running of a limited company are necessarily strict, and you will need to invest a little time and effort in learning how to abide by them.

At the time of going to press, all private limited companies need at least one officially named director and an official company secretary. However this is due to change under the government's Company Law Reform Bill, introduced in November 2005, which has recommended that the requirement for a company secretary in a private company is abolished. This is unlikely to be made law before April 2007 though.

The director's responsibilities include managing the company in accordance with current law and the company's Articles of Association. The company secretary's responsibilities include the handling of official administration and ensuring that paperwork is filed with Companies House as and when required. If a company has just one director, then the company secretary must be a separate individual. However, where two or more directors are appointed, one of them is allowed to serve as the company secretary as well.

It is important to avoid confusing a private limited company, which we have just discussed, with a public limited company, or PLC. A public limited company works in much the same way as a private limited company, but its shares are available to the general public via the stock exchange. Before a PLC can commence business, it must prove to Companies House that it has issued at least £50,000 worth of shares, as well as meeting other miscellaneous criteria.

The trading status you choose to go with as you launch your business is a matter of personal preference and will also depend on how much potential there will be for liability. If you want to start a business simply and quickly, and are unlikely to borrow heavily or expose yourself to liabilities, the sole trader or partnership route may be most suitable. However, if you are prepared to take care of a little paperwork in order to establish a more 'impressive' status, or if you may need to limit your personal liability, setting up a private limited company may be more appropriate. As always, it is a good idea to discuss your needs with a professional advisor before making a final decision.

We didn't have any preconceptions about what shape or form our business would take legally, until the opportunity arose for business angels to invest in it. At that point we had to create a limited liability company so that the investors could buy shares in it.

SHOULD YOU SELL EQUITY IN YOUR BUSINESS?

Many people are reluctant to consider selling shares in their business initially. They see it as their baby – something that they are risking a heck of a lot for, so why should an outsider get a piece of the action? We have always believed that in our particular case, it is better to own 80 per cent of something rather than 100 per cent of nothing. Bringing in outside investors will obviously mean more money, but it should also mean bringing in more knowledge, skills and experience to the business. As an owner/manager or entrepreneur you are constantly discovering new things you are capable of or good at, but you also discover your own limitations. If your staff don't stick around, your new business is suffering or your accounts aren't adding up, then you need to look at your ability as a people manager, commercial director and financial planner. External investors such as business angels or venture capitalists should strengthen your business, because they will undoubtedly be bringing their skills to the table which will complement and strengthen your own.

GET THE BASICS: SELLING COMPANY SHARES TO RAISE EQUITY FINANCE

One advantage of setting up your business as a private limited company (as opposed to operating as a sole trader or partnership) is that it enables you to sell shares in the company to third-party investors in order to raise equity finance. The word 'equity' in business means much the same as it does in the world of property: the cash value of the business after all claims against it have been deducted. The more profitable a business is, the more equity it has. A business that is valued at £50,000 and has debts of £15,000 would therefore have an equity value of £35,000, and you could effectively sell part of this equity by issuing shares.

Consider the following scenario. You start a private limited company with £1,000 which is divided into 1,000 × £1 ordinary shares. Because you invested all £1,000 in the company, you would start out as the sole shareholder of the company. However, you don't have to remain the sole shareholder if you don't want to. You could allocate a certain number of shares to be issued (that is, sold) to outside investors. There are a number of advantages to taking this course of action:

★ Selling shares enables you to recoup some of your original investment in the company.

★ The money realised by selling shares doesn't constitute a loan, so you won't have to repay the money or pay interest on it.

★ Selling shares isn't difficult, as long as you have people who wish to buy them. There will be some paperwork and communication with Companies House involved, but your accountant will be able to guide you through all of that without too much difficulty.

Of course, there are also some disadvantages to selling shares in your company:

★ The people who buy shares are buying part ownership of the company itself. Investors are therefore entitled to attend shareholder meetings and have a say (however small) in how the business is run. The more shares an investor owns, the more influence he or she can have on the company.

★ As part-owners of your business, shareholders are entitled to a portion of the profit it makes. These sums are payable via share dividends that are distributed to shareholders.

★ If you sell more than 50 per cent of the shares in your company, you effectively lose overall control of the company itself, and could be voted off the board of directors.

It is important to note that selling shares in a private limited company is not the same as floating a company on the Stock Exchange. Company flotation is a lot more complicated and not at all suitable for many businesses. You should also note that issuing ordinary shares in a private limited company is not always the best way to raise finance for your business. For these reasons, it is essential that you discuss the idea of raising equity finance with your accountant, who will advise you according to your unique situation and circumstances.

Business angels

When we were first setting up the Gapwork business, we knew that we could do with help on the financial and legal side of things. So we went to the Yorkshire Association of Business Angels and got the chance to present to a room full of potential investors. Initially we saw it as an opportunity to find a financial advisor who might be able to help us write a full business plan, but on the spur of the moment we decided to ask for just enough money to set the website up and pay us for a few months to dedicate our time fully to the project.

REBECCA SAYS:

I don't remember being nervous, but we must have been, as the investors were almost all male, over the age of 40 and dressed in suits. The other businesses presenting that night included ones that were already turning over lots of money, and they all had very impressive PowerPoint presentations. We, by comparison, had prepared a single-sided sheet of notes about our website idea to read from and that was about it. What we tried to convey in our presentation was the simplicity of the idea, the need in the market and some basic numbers. We didn't claim that we would be able to turn over a million within the first year, or even in the first three years. We simply shared our vision simply and honestly. At the end of the presentation we met a handful of investors who were interested, and they decided to put money into the business on the basis of an equity share.

TOP TIPS FOR PRESENTING TO BUSINESS ANGELS

(contributed by Barbara Greaves, David Marsh and Peter Ball from the Yorkshire Association of Business Angels)

★ Make your first shot a good one.
★ Prepare your presentation thoroughly and practise it in front of friends, family or anyone who will sit still long enough.
★ Make sure you don't overrun the allotted time.
★ Be prepared for rejection.
★ Be prepared to 'sell' part of your company (it's better to have 50 per cent of a multi-million pound company than 100 per cent of an idea).
★ Sell yourself – your skills, drive and enthusiasm count for a lot.
★ Remember that angels invest in the person as much, if not more, than the product or service you intend to provide.
★ Describe the product or service clearly, without being too technical, and don't use jargon.
★ Highlight your management team strengths (if you have a management team).
★ Demonstrate market potential, but be realistic.
★ Demonstrate how and when you will make your first and subsequent sales.
★ Identify skills and advice you would be looking for from the angels.
★ Confirm how much you need, what it's for and when you need it.
★ Make sure that you 'gel' with the angel or lead angel of a syndicate.
★ If possible, confirm a possible exit route and a timescale.

Valuing the company wasn't difficult for us, as we knew it was too early to put a value on anything. We sold the angels 15 per cent for £15,000. This might sound like a lot of shares for not a lot of cash, but as we said earlier, all we had at the time was an idea and nothing to lose. We were very focused on the exit route for the investors, and showed them how they would be making a clear profit within a three-year period. By selling some equity we had enough cash to get the website up and running, and to pay our (miniscule) salaries for a few months. So much for hitting the jackpot!

Having a low level of investment in a business usually means that the business is under-resourced, which can hinder its growth. But it also means that it's sink or swim for those at the coal face. Either your idea works and you can break even, or it doesn't and you go bust. It's a gamble, but only as big a gamble as you want to make it. Our investors knew that an untested idea developed by two young, relatively inexperienced people was a big gamble, so they minimised their risk by only investing a small amount of cash. The angels went on to invest a further £20,000 in the business, in return for 20 per cent of the shares. The key thing for us was that we retained majority shares, having agreed beforehand that we wouldn't sell more than 50 per cent.

Getting money from the banks

Getting by on a minimal amount of capital can be frustrating. When we first set up we worked from home, on a home computer and with a home landline. We bought office furniture from a junk shop around the corner. The investors wanted to keep an eye on their money, so one of them did our monthly management accounts and ran the board meetings. He was also secretary and chairman. Every penny we spent we had to run past him first. It soon became clear that in order to enable the business to grow, we would need further investment. We didn't want to part with any more equity, so we needed to look at loans or grants.

We needed more cash than any grants could offer us, so we talked to banks about loans. If we had owned property at this point, or anything of value, then we could have got a secured bank loan. However, our lack of collateral meant that our only real option was to look at unsecured loans. Neither of us wanted to get into personal debt for the sake of trying our business idea, even if we could have got an unsecured personal loan (a lack of steady income and student debts meant that we weren't exactly a lender's dream customer), so we looked into the Small Firms Loan Guarantee Scheme (SFLGS). This is a source of business funding mostly underwritten by the Department of Trade and Industry and given out by high street banks.

Backed by our angels, we approached a number of local banks with our carefully polished business plan in hand. We thought that having obtained investment from business angels and sponsorship from high street brands, our business would be perfect for a scheme which claimed to open doors for start-ups. We knew that we met the eligibility criteria, so when we had our first meeting with our own friendly bank manager who was very positive, we were pleased. Soon after that meeting, the friendly bank manager left and our next meeting was with her replacement. He was our new business advisor and looked at our business plan as if it was a drawing of a space alien done by a five year old. His attitude was superbly condescending, considering he looked barely old enough to serve drinks in a pub. He picked holes in the plan and rejected it as too far fetched to be eligible for funding. We were gutted, but took the plan to two or three other banks, all of whom gave us a similar response. Our investors were furious and pulled out all the stops on the old boys' network to get the plan in front of someone more senior at our own bank. He liked the look of the business and said he would support an SFLGS application.

To be frank, we were horrified by the attitude of the high street banks that we had approached. The SFLGS is underwritten to the tune of 75 per cent by the Department of Trade and Industry. We had applied for £25,000, so the banks would only actually have been risking £6,250 of their own money on our loan. It doesn't do much for the confidence of a start-up entrepreneur when the bank effectively says that it wouldn't even bet just over £6K on your business succeeding. Especially when you have to pay for set-up fees and insurance on the loan – both of which provide pure profit for the bank itself.

The bank loan myth

We have since learned that we shouldn't have been horrified by the attitude of high street banks. We shouldn't even have been surprised. The key thing to bear in mind when approaching banks for funding is that they are not really funding or investment institutions for start-up businesses. High street banks are there as repositories for your money. They are not there to risk money by giving unsecured loans to limited companies.

Of course, that's not the picture they like to paint in their glossy advertising brochures and television commercials. Banks want people to think that they're everyone's best friend and their customers' most loyal advocates. But, at the end of the day, they are banks because they are good at holding onto money, not gambling with it.

So, if this is the case, where *can* you get the money you need to start your business?

GET THE BASICS: FUNDING YOUR BUSINESS

All businesses need money to get started or expand, and few people have adequate savings personally to cover all the costs involved. This means that most have to secure at least some external funding somewhere along the line, and this can be done in a number of ways. The most common options when it comes to funding a business are detailed below.

Private loans

Many businesses are launched with the help of loans obtained from friends and family members. While this is a perfectly viable route to take (especially if you happen to have incredibly wealthy relatives), it is not without its drawbacks:

★ You will feel under more pressure to ensure that the business does well. Starting a business can be stressful enough as it is, but when you are working with money borrowed from friends and relatives, this stress can be much worse.

★ Your personal relationships with the people you borrow from could become strained if the business does not perform as well expected.

If you do decide to borrow money from friends or relatives to finance a business start-up, make sure that you spell out the risks involved in the arrangement and consider what you will do if the business doesn't succeed. Then, if everyone still wants to go ahead, draw up a formal agreement in writing. You might not think that you need anything in writing right now, but it's prudent to be on the safe side all the same.

Bank loans

Another way of raising finance for a new venture is to apply for a business loan from a regular high street bank. While our experience indicates that banks only tend to lend money to people who don't really need it, it is still true that many businesses have benefited from bank loans. If you have a forward-thinking bank manager (which, it has to be said, is quite a find) then he or she is likely to be just as interested in your business plan as he is about how much security you have. For this reason, it's always worth applying for a business loan even if all you have is a good idea and a solid business plan to back it up. You never know, your own local bank manager could be one of the good ones!

Applying for a bank loan usually involves meeting the business manager to discuss your needs and then completing an application form. Sometimes the manager can approve a loan on the spot – especially if the amount requested is fairly modest – but otherwise you can expect to be given a decision within ten working days or so.

Small firms loan guarantee

For businesses that have tried to get a conventional loan and failed because they don't have enough security, or their bank manager is just too short-sighted to give the required stamp of approval, the Small Firms Loan Guarantee scheme (operated by the Department of Trade and Industry) will guarantee loans in return for an annual premium equal to 2 per cent of the outstanding loan. Loans of between £5,000 and £100,000 are available (£250,000 if the business has been running for more than two years) on terms of between two and ten years.

Only companies in the UK qualify for this scheme, and they must have an annual turnover of less than £3 million (£5 million if it's a manufacturing business). There are also several exclusions and restrictions which need to be considered before application. For further details, visit **www.dti.gov.uk/sflg** online or request further information by phone on 0870 1502500. You can also write to: DTI Enquiry Unit, 1 Victoria Street, London, SW1H 0ET.

The Prince's Trust

If you are aged 18–30, currently unemployed (or work less than 16 hours per week) and have failed to raise finance with a bank for your business idea, The Prince's Trust may offer you a low interest start-up loan of up to £4,000 (£5,000 if you are looking to operate as a partnership). Grants of up to £1,500 are sometimes offered 'in special circumstances'. Because the trust does not have unlimited resources (who does?), applications are 'assessed on their individual merits' and preference is given to the eligible applicants who need help the most.

The first step in applying for support from The Prince's Trust is to complete an online enquiry form on the website (**www.princes-trust.org.uk**) or to call 0800 842 842 to be put in touch with your nearest office.

Equity finance

For businesses that are already established, equity finance is another way to raise extra money. The basic idea is that you allow someone to invest in your business and, in return, you give them a share of the business itself. There are two main sources of equity finance:

★ Business angels are individual investors. Because they draw on their personal wealth, business angels tend to invest infrequently and often in areas that they are experienced in.

★ Venture capital is provided by companies that specialise in funding the expansion of large businesses. They are generally only interested in businesses that need an injection of £2 million or more.

Two advantages of obtaining equity finance are that, unlike loans, it has no fixed repayment deadline and interest is not payable on the amount invested in the business. Instead, the investor usually receives dividend payments related to the profitability of the business. Another advantage is that the investors have a personal interest in seeing the business succeed and prosper, because they obviously want their investment to grow in value.

Of course, there are disadvantages too. The main one is the fact that part of the business will be owned by the outside investors. They may also want to take control of (or at least have a say in) how the business is run once they are involved.

However you choose to go about raising finance, your business plan will play a key role in determining whether or not you are successful. So, if you haven't done so already, take time to make sure that you have a business plan which is as strong as possible before you approach a bank or any other lender.

It is worth bearing in mind that many businesses are started without investment from traditional institutions. The two businesses below found alternative ways of funding their ideas.

While travelling in different countries, I wondered why I could not find such lovely, different kitchen and dining products in the UK. This inspired me to launch **www,kitchengoddess.co.uk**, a website selling really gorgeous kitchen and table accessories for women who like entertaining in the comfort of their own homes.

Having put together my business plan, I went to get some expert financial advice from the bank as well as from Business Link. I'd calculated that I needed around £10k to launch, which included building and hosting the website, marketing, designing my logo and purchasing equipment. I had some savings but I needed a loan too.

My bank manager offered me a business loan, but it was very expensive compared to the personal loan rates you see advertised everywhere. This was really off-putting and I knew it would be a risky option, especially if things were slow to start with.

The Business Link advisor suggested we should look at grants. We went through the whole list of grants available but none seemed to fit my profile. I was beginning to think that I would have to take the more expensive route of the business loan from the bank when the advisor came up with the bright idea of approaching a local charity, called the Harry James Riddleston Charity. Harry, a local entrepreneur who started his own business life with very little capital, decided to use his wealth to set up a charitable trust to help young people make a start in the world of business by offering a limited number of interest-free loans.

This seemed like the perfect route. Following application forms, reference checks and an interview with the trustees,

I was very fortunate and very grateful that the charity felt as confident in my idea as I did and granted my business a five-year, interest-free loan. This significantly bolstered the capital I had saved and has definitely taken a lot of pressure off in these early days. The whole experience was really positive; I think they could see my passion and that convinced them!

CHLOE BEALE OF TALIA THEATRE

Talia Theatre began on a busy street in Belgium, where we started our street theatre career, living for a year on what we found in our hat at the end of each performance. When we returned to England after an extremely inspiring and exciting time travelling Europe, we were keen to give the company a more official standing. We then registered with Companies House, designed our letter head etc. We also applied for our first grant from the then North West Arts Board. It was a small grant of up to £5,000 called 'Arts for Everyone' – and that is basically what it was: pretty much anyone who could fill in the application could apply for it.

From this point on we began to build our relationship with the Arts Council. However, for this relationship to be successful, the Council needed to see our work. So over the next three years, we created a huge amount of work with very little money and a lot of hard graft. We performed wherever and whenever, often doing shows for free if it meant the right people would see us. This paid off when the Arts Council agreed to fund us for three years.

Simultaneously we had been developing our relationship with Blackburn and Darwen Borough Council, where our community work was beginning to attract European social and regeneration money; we worked with most local primary schools and all the secondary schools, as well as over 500 socially excluded adults.

Of course we constantly apply for individual pots of money where appropriate. Having never been core funded, we have always suffered from a sense of insecurity which has been hard to manage. Now our successful partnership with Proper Job has given us the opportunity to develop further into the next exciting phase.

Visit Proper Job online at: www.properjob.org.uk

It pays to do a bit of blue-sky thinking when it comes to finding money. Brainstorm as many ways as possible of raising cash – no matter how outlandish. You would be surprised what you can find when you start looking beyond the banks.

How much will your business cost?
Look after the pennies . . .

Think of all the trappings that you would associate with successful business people – the swanky office space, leather sofas in the foyer, attractive plants strategically placed, a glamorous receptionist, bubbling water coolers, top-of-the-range computers, coffee makers, modern art on the walls, busy assistants, chic suits, fancy BMW or Mercedes parked in a named space outside the building, expense accounts, slick hotels, an expensive logo on smooth matt stationery, overseas trips in first class cabins – and now forget it all.

Welcome to the world of SME (small to medium-sized enterprises) start-ups. This is the real world, where you start off working from your front room because you can't afford an office. You drive an old banger because what money you are making is being ploughed back into the business. You go on business trips and beg sofa space from friends who you haven't had time to see socially for months. You kick yourself every time you forget to take headed paper out of the printer when you just need to print out an e-mail. Your working wardrobe consists of whatever you had left over from your old life, cast-offs from friends with proper jobs and stuff you have picked up in the sales. You look forward to networking events not because of the opportunity they offer to make new contacts, but because you get free food and drink and it means you don't have to find the energy to cook for yourself that night. Every overseas phone call has an annoying prefix to dial before the main number, and the nearest you get to first class on an aircraft or train is when you walk past it on the way to the cheap seats.

This is the harsh reality for most start-up businesses – and we believe that it is a healthy reality. Businesses such as those set up in the dot-com boom of the 1990s, which had enormous amounts of initial investment, are on shaky foundations. They had such huge overheads that all their funding was spent on 'brand building', leasing expensive city centre offices and the expense accounts of their directors. These things are all well and good, if prioritised properly. But without a strong team, a solid product or service to offer and a clear channel to reach an obvious target market, a business will fail, regardless of the initial investment.

The key thing is to be realistic about what you need to get your business up and running, and how you will then sustain it (or how it will sustain you) in the early days. Your financial projections might be telling you that you will have nothing to worry about, but it is vital that you don't overestimate sales and underestimate costs. Otherwise your business could go belly up very quickly. You should therefore balance a conservative, realistic sales forecast with trying to trim costs wherever possible. Ask yourself the following questions:

★ Do you need an office? If you do, does it have to be 'client facing'? That is, does it need to have a nice reception area and meeting rooms, or will a cheaper, more basic alternative do?

★ Can you beg or borrow (not steal!) things that you need? You would be amazed at how many people (especially if they are already running their own business) will have old but perfectly adequate PCs, phones and other office equipment lying around unused.

★ Can you call in favours? Don't be shy – if you know designers who could create a logo, stationery or even a website, ask them if they would be willing to do it on the cheap, as a contra-deal (that is, you help them out with something you have that they want) or even for free (depending on how cheeky you are).

★ Do you need state-of-the-art equipment? If you are a designer or work in IT, then it is likely that you will need computers etc which are pretty high spec. But if you aren't, don't worry about spending a fortune on the latest equipment. If all you need is an e-mail address, a phone line and a word processor, then you won't need anything different to what you would use at home.

★ Do you need a Public Relations agency? In our experience, no. One of the most common mistakes a start-up business can make is to rely on PR as a driver for sales. We found that sales are not driven by having an article in the local paper. It may be different for other businesses, but paying an agency a retainer is an expensive way of finding out that it won't work. A more cost-effective option (if you are convinced that PR is valuable for your business) would be to find a good freelancer, who will work out as better value for money. And don't tie yourself into any minimum-term contracts.

★ Do you need a fancy car and designer clothes to make an impact? No. A good rule of thumb is to dress the way in which you want to be perceived by others, but don't make the mistake of thinking that you need to look like a corporate big-hitter to make people take you seriously. And driving a car which is flashier than those of your clients can give out the wrong signals.

★ Do you need staff? If you absolutely do need staff when you are setting up, make sure that you are paying them at the right level. You can check this by using a salary checker like the one at http:// content.monster.co.uk/salarychecker. You should also make sure that you are not paying someone less than the national minimum wage by going to www.dti.gov.uk/er/nmw.

GET THE BASICS: COSTING YOUR BUSINESS
When it comes to figuring out how much money your business will need, you can't afford to be vague. Instead, you need

to roll up your sleeves and go through all of the various aspects of the business carefully, being sure not to overlook things that aren't so obvious, such as tax and promotional expenses.

To help you go through this process, we will now take you through a list of the main things that almost all businesses need to consider from a costing point of view.

Staff costs

It's a fact of life that people aren't usually willing to work for free, so start by calculating how much your business will need to pay for staff. Include any part-time employees you plan on hiring (for example, cleaners) as well as full-time. If you aren't sure how much you should pay people, look for similar jobs advertised in the newspapers or local employment centre to get ball-park figures. Don't forget to include 'hidden' staff costs such as employers' National Insurance contributions and any company pension contributions you might make. And, of course, don't forget to include your own salary when costing this section! It isn't straightforward estimating how much you should pay yourself as an owner/manager of a business – you don't want the business to suffer because you are paying yourself too much. On the other hand, you have to make sure that you are covering your mortgage and essential bills.

Rent and rates

The amount of money required to pay for rent and rates is usually quite substantial. If you know the exact figures involved in your particular venture, that's great. Otherwise, find out what other businesses in your desired location are paying (local estate agencies are often a good place to go for this kind of information) and use a fair average as your own estimate.

Bills

No matter what kind of business you are setting up, it will generate an assortment of bills that you need to plan for. Electricity, gas, telephone lines, Internet connections and water supplies all cost money, so don't overlook these things when calculating how much your business will need.

Marketing

All businesses need to market their products and services, whether it's through advertising, billboards, direct mailings or a particularly snazzy website. You should estimate not only how much money you will need to market your business at launch, but also how much you intend to spend on marketing on an ongoing basis. Bear in mind the 'hidden costs' of marketing that might be involved. For example, radio advertising not only involves paying for air time, but it might also involve hiring a copywriter to script the commercial and paying production costs on top of that.

Stationery

Pens, pencils, receipt rolls, fax rolls, carrier bags, notebooks, accounts books, reams of paper and ink cartridges for a printer all cost money. Individually you might not think that any of these things are expensive enough to be worth worrying about, but collectively they can cost a surprisingly substantial amount. To price these things accurately, obtain a catalogue from a stationery supplies company such as Viking Direct, which is online at **www.viking-direct.co.uk**.

Equipment

Obtaining the equipment required to set up any kind of business is usually a relatively expensive task. Of course, it could be that you already have some of the equipment you need (for example, you may already have a personal computer that you can use for business purposes), but everything else needs to be bought and paid for at the outset. Estimate the cost of purchasing by using average high street prices, but remember to shop around for the best possible deals when it actually comes to putting your money down.

Insurance policies

All businesses need insurance. You will need to insure your premises, your vehicles, your equipment and your stock. You will also need to take out public liability insurance in case anyone should ever make a claim against you (for example, because they injure themselves whilst visiting your premises). Getting reliable estimate figures for all of these insurances is often as easy as going online and obtaining a few quotes from different companies.

Travel

If your business will involve travelling on a regular basis, include costs such as petrol, parking, train tickets, hotel bills and tube fares. Even a weekly trip to the local cash and carry can create a hefty petrol bill over the course of a year, so it's important to take even these 'minor' travelling expenses into account.

Research

Some businesses involve an element of research. For example, a restaurant might need to investigate how the general public would react to a new establishment specialising in Indian, Chinese, French or Cantonese food. This research will need to be paid for, so don't overlook it, even if it's not something that will be ongoing.

Promotions

Promotions are a great way to attract new clients and keep existing ones happy. But whether it's giving away free key fobs and balloons to anyone who visits a store during the opening week, or offering a 20 per cent discount on all new contracts, someone needs to pay for the promotion – and that someone is you. Budget for promotions from the beginning and you won't make the mistake of going overboard.

Public relations

There are many ways of maintaining good relationships with the general public. Some businesses set up free telephone helplines for their customers. Others sponsor charitable events and organisations. Still others hire copywriters to write press releases and public information materials on a regular basis. PR consultants and agencies charge a 'retainer' for their services, which means that you have to pay out on a monthly basis. You can get quotes from agencies and freelancers to give you an idea of costs. If you intend to do any of these things, estimate the cost involved at the outset.

Advisors

Accountants, solicitors and other professional advisors are famous for their sizeable fees, and most businesses use them on at least an annual basis. Figure this into your costing exercise so that you don't get a nasty surprise later on.

Tax

Although it's obviously difficult to say how much you will have to pay in tax until you have a fairly solid idea about how much profit your business will make, you can and should make rough estimates. Many businesses use a third of estimated profit as a general rule of thumb, and this seems to work out quite well.

By taking all these elements into account, you will get a much more accurate idea of how much money your business will need, not just to set up in the first place, but to keep it running smoothly over the long term.

MANAGING YOUR MONEY

So what happens when you do get some investment capital together, or you do finally take the plunge and take out that loan? When you are starting your own business it is tempting to see everything in terms of 'When I do this, then it will get easier'. So you might say to yourself, 'When I get some funding together, then I will be able to hire staff, and when I hire staff, my workload won't be so massive and it will all get easier'. If only this were the case. We will discuss the subject of staff a little later, but for now, let's tackle the issue of actually managing your money.

Nothing prepares you for having to manage cash flow as part of your business. Even if you have been a finance director for a big company, the pressures are very different when it is your own cash that you are having to spend. This is why, in a way, it is better to start with a little and learn how to manage that effectively. If we had been given a million pounds to start Gapwork, we wouldn't have had the first idea about what to do with it all. As it was, we had £15,000, which we used to pay ourselves a small wage for a few months and to pay for things that were essential for our business. One of our business angels was a chartered accountant and helped us to learn quickly how important proper accounting practices are. It is vital that you understand the difference between profit and loss and a cash flow sheet, for starters. Let's pause to consider these things before continuing.

A CRASH COURSE IN ELECTRONIC BOOK-KEEPING

Decades ago, keeping the financial side of even a small business in order could be a real pain. Various cash books and ledgers needed to be kept and checked manually. If you were lucky, you might have had a desk calculator to help you out, but even then it was common for a person to press the wrong button and have to start over again.

Fortunately, basic accounting in the modern age is a great deal easier, thanks to that marvel of modern technology, the personal computer, and special business accounting software packages such as those provided by Sage or Quicken. As long as you have a PC and one of these software applications, then keeping your books in order is as simple as following a few basic principles:

Maintain a cash book

Create a cash book file and use this to record the details of all income and outgoings. Each item should be dated and categorised. For example, if you spend £50 on filling the company van with petrol, you should enter the date and the £50 expenditure, and categorise the whole transaction under something like, 'Business Expense: Motor : Petrol'. Almost all modern software packages allow you to create a number of categories once so that you can simply 'file' new transactions under the appropriate heading as you enter them.

Because you enter both income and outgoings into the cash book, it effectively gives you an accurate running total of how your business is doing at any given time. If the balance of the cash book is positive, then you're in profit. If it's negative, you're making a loss. Of course, it's only accurate if you keep it updated regularly.

Don't forget that you need to keep all receipts pertaining to your business expenses for at least seven years to comply with the tax laws in the UK. You should also keep copies of all invoices issued. This is so that the Inland Revenue have a clear 'paper trail' that it can use to verify your accounts, if the need arises.

Create a sales ledger and purchase ledger

These are two separate files which tend to be used by businesses when invoicing. In the Sales Ledger, you record details of the sales that you make, including the date of the transaction, a brief description of the product or service sold and the number of the invoice issued. Then, when outstanding invoices are paid, you note the date of receipt alongside the relevant transaction.

In the Purchase Ledger, you record details of purchases that you make from your suppliers. Once again, you should include the date of the transaction, a brief description of the product or service purchased and the number of the invoice that has been issued to you. Then, when you settle an invoice, you make a note of the date of payment alongside the relevant transaction.

Sales and purchase ledgers enable you to know exactly where you stand in terms of the money you owe to your suppliers and the money that is owed to you from your own clients.

Once you have got into the habit of entering this kind of information into your PC on a regular basis, you will find that most modern accounting packages will create all the other reports you need at the touch of a button. This is very handy, as it means that you can leave your PC to crunch the numbers and print out a nice clean profit and loss statement for your accountant each year, or a VAT report which will help you to submit your quarterly VAT return to HM Customs.

The profit and loss statement

The profit and loss statement is one which summarises the financial activity of your business over a given period. It does this by listing sub-totals for each of the categories in your cash book, and then totalling all of these categories to give you incoming and outgoing figures. The statement then shows the difference between total income and total outgoings. If the former exceeds the latter, the statement will show a profit. If it's the other way around, the statement will obviously show a loss. Hence the name – profit and loss statement.

The VAT report

If you tell your accounting software to 'tag' transactions with the correct VAT codes, then every quarter you can get your PC to print out a VAT report. This will show the figures that you need to enter on your VAT return before submitting to HM Customs. If you aren't registered for VAT, then this is no big deal. But if you are, this feature can save you several hours – and the printout can be filed so that you have something to refer to if there's ever a query about your returns in the future.

Of course, we aren't suggesting here that a PC with the right software can totally replace an accountant, because it can't. And you always need to remember that your PC accounts will only ever be as accurate as you are when it comes to inputting your figures. However, if you are careful to maintain accuracy and use your PC effectively, the reports it provides can make your accountant's job a great deal easier – and this will help to reduce his or her fees to a minimum. Just don't forget to keep back-up copies of all your data!

In addition to knowing our cash book from our ledgers, we also learned the importance of accurate and regular financial reporting. When our business started, Kirsty (as the commercial and financial half of our partnership) was able to process financial information herself using basic accountancy software. Our angel investor would oversee things and complete the management accounts. However, as the business grew, Kirsty was better equipped for strategic financial planning and we needed to find a bookkeeper who would be able to track sales, send out invoices, do the pay roll, sort out our VAT and record our expenses.

After a couple of trials and errors (including one bookkeeper who insisted on carrying £50,000 worth of invoices around in her rucksack to and from the office), we found a part-qualified accountant/bookkeeper who was able to handle the particular quirks of our business. This is a really key thing. If you don't feel 100 per cent happy with handling and understanding the financials of your business, then find someone who does. There are people in this world who like nothing better than inputting figures, doing sums and getting a warm glow of satisfaction when their books balance. They are the bookkeepers and accountants of this world and eventually your business should be given the benefit of their expertise, unless you are absolutely convinced that you are doing the best possible job. The best thing about these financial wizards is that they don't necessarily want to be employed by you – they will work on a part-time basis, doing as many hours as you need them to. They also won't cost the earth. A small business doesn't need a 'big four' accountancy firm to watch over their finances.

At the same time it is vital that you get to grips with the incomings and outgoings of your own business. When you have your business up and running, you should be able to reel off the answers to the following questions at any given moment:

★ How much has the business got in the bank?
★ How much do you owe to suppliers/creditors?
★ When is your next big tax bill and how much will it be?
★ How much money are you owed by debtors?
★ When is this money due to come in?
★ What is your projected turnover by the end of the year?
★ How much profit will you make by the end of the year?
★ Are you on track so far?

If you can't answer any of these questions instantly, then you need to get your head around your financials.

Systems need to be set in place so that at the end of every week you have a basic update of what's come in, what's gone out and what is pending. You should then have a monthly set of accounts which tell you what has happened over the month. At the end of the year, you will have a full set of accounts which will give you a clear picture of how your business has developed. As well as weekly and monthly reporting, you should have your business plan figures which include your profit and loss and cash flow projections. These will give you an idea of what you have coming up in the future. Without all this information you run the risk of running your business 'blind' and this is when something nasty and unexpected could crop up.

Having a year's worth of figures is useful because you can spot potentially vulnerable situations which may be avoidable. For example, you may have a strong seasonality to your business which isn't ideal (for us this involves schools buying resources at certain times of the year). Alternatively, you may realise when you look back that you were paying all year for something which you only used for a few months. It is numbers that will tell you these things, so don't be scared of them.

It can be difficult for people who are running a business based on something that they love, or are passionate about, to get to grips with the fact that businesses live or die not on the enthusiasm of their owner/manager, or on how worthwhile the cause is, but on cash flow. All those clichés, particularly 'turnover is vanity, profit is sanity and cash flow is king', are absolutely right, whether you like it not.

TO SUM UP . . .

★ Reduce your financial risk wherever possible and practical.
★ Choose your trading status carefully.
★ Look at all the funding options that are open to you.
★ Have a handle on your costs at all times.
★ Outsource your financial reporting if you aren't comfortable with it, but make sure you know what money is coming in, what is going out and how much you have in the bank at any given time.

WRITING A BUSINESS PLAN

When you are working in a 'normal' job, you rarely have to write a plan for something over a one- or even three-year timescale. When you are starting your own business, it's a different matter. The success of your business relies on doing some written planning. Planning is important for other reasons too. You need a plan to work out whether you are going to make money for one thing, and against which to plot your progress. You will also need a plan to show to potential investors and your bank, and to help you understand the direction your business should take.

When we realised we would need a business plan, we searched on the Internet and contacted large firms of accountants, who produce helpful and free guides to writing a business plan. The plan which we produced to show the business angels back in 1999 was by no means comprehensive, but it was enough to help them see what we were aiming to do and that it was realistic. Indeed, that was the key thing which they liked about the business – the fact that the plan was realistic, conservative even. A business plan is only as good as the logic and figures which go into it, and an over-ambitious plan will look unrealistic to even the most casual reader.

We knew that our plan was basic and unpolished. But one of the main reasons we presented to the business angels in the first place was that we wanted someone to come on board as a financial director so that they could help us write a better plan. We knew about the market and our products, but we didn't know much at all about the cash flow projections or profit and loss sheets that were required. Remember that while there are plenty of accountants, consultants, software packages and business support organisations who will help you to structure the financial section of your business plan, you need to get to grips with the figures that are going into it. Know your numbers!

GET THE BASICS: WHY WRITE A BUSINESS PLAN?
You know what a business plan is and you know the kind of things that it covers. But what's the point of writing one?

Well, there are several very good reasons for taking the time:

1 To clarify your idea

Writing down your idea in a detailed, carefully structured way that covers the basic concept, your marketing approach, the 'nuts and bolts' of running the business and financial forecasts is one of the best possible ways to gain overall clarity. By forcing yourself to sit down and think through every aspect of your business, you sharpen your intentions and the initial 'good idea' is gradually transformed into a realistic and workable action plan. At this stage, the idea becomes a much more concrete statement of intention, and the chances of you making it a reality soar.

2 To test your projections

When it comes to things like deciding how much to charge for a product or service, or how much you can afford to spend on raw materials and other overheads, it's easy to fall into the trap of being overly optimistic or, worse, excessively vague. Drawing up a business plan allows you to get right down to the nitty gritty specifics and test your financial projections in advance, so you can assess whether or not your figures are likely to be workable in the real world. And if they aren't, you can revise them until they are!

3 To attract investors and partners

If you want to attract investors and/or partners to your business, having a solid plan which shows exactly what the business is all about will be a massive help. Having the idea fleshed out in black and white will make it far more appealing and workable than relating it verbally ever could.

4 To secure finance from a bank

If you will need to secure finance from a bank (for example, via a business start-up loan), then you will find that showing the bank a clear and detailed business plan is usually a compulsory requirement. Banks tend to lend money only to those individuals and businesses that will, in their judgement, be able to pay it back without much difficulty. If your business plan demonstrates that you have thought things through carefully and realistically, the chances of you securing bank finance are much greater than they would be otherwise.

WHAT YOUR BUSINESS PLAN SHOULD CONTAIN

A business plan is a carefully structured 'road map' which shows anyone who looks at it what your business is all about and how you intend to make it work. There are many different variations on this basic theme, but most business plans cover at least six vital areas in six distinct sections:

1 The intention statement or executive summary

This is where you state the basic vision for your business as specifically as you can. Not only should you provide a summary of what product or service you intend to offer, but you should also say who you are targeting as customers. For example, 'Mama Mia's Muffins will sell luxurious Italian muffins from a permanent stand in Bluewater shopping centre. We will focus on serving Bluewater visitors who want a tasty snack at the time of purchase, and also those who want to take a boxed batch of muffins home as a family treat'. It is crucial to get this part of the plan right, as if an investor doesn't have time to read the full document, he or she will just scan the intention statement to get an idea of whether the business is interesting or not.

2 A detailed description

Having conveyed the gist of your business idea, the detailed description section should go into more depth. For example, what will be your operating hours? How many days each week? How many varieties of muffin will you offer? How will they be presented to customers? You also need to say what makes your business different or better than similar ones already in the area. For example, are your muffins healthier, cheaper, more tasty or more attractively packaged?

3 Your marketing strategy

How will you market your business? Through radio advertising? Newspaper ads? Word of mouth? By using a particularly eye-catching stand? This section needs to show that you've planned your marketing campaign in some detail.

4 Personnel

In this section, tell the reader who will be involved in running the business. Who will serve customers? Who will do the administration? Who will source the product? For each person named, say a little about why they will be able to handle the job. For example, if Mary will be making Mama Mia's Muffins and she also made muffins for a large bakery for ten years, say so. You will need to go into detail about your past history, why you are setting up this business and what your relevant experience is.

5 Logistics

This is where you present the 'nuts and bolts' of how the business will operate on a day-to-day basis. For example, where exactly will you get the muffins from? If you are going to bake your own, where will you do this? How many will you bake each day? Where will your ingredients come from? How many customers will you be able to serve in a typical hour, or day? The more detail you can provide here, the better.

6 Financial forecasts

In this section of the business plan, you should explain how much it will take to launch the business, how much of this you will need to borrow (if any) and how much you intend to spend on wages, rent, bills, marketing and everything else that has costs associated with it. You also need to include:

★ **A cashflow statement for the first year or two. This should show how much cash you expect to have available on a month-by-month basis.**

★ **A profit and loss statement showing how much money you expect to generate from sales, how much you expect to spend on overheads (rates, cost of raw materials, etc) and how much profit you would have if both estimates translate to actual operating figures.**

The financial forecasts are the most important part of any business plan and are the bits which you should know inside out. If you are not confident with figures, there are plenty of sources of help available. You could pay an accountant to work with you on the figures, or get some free advice from your bank manager. For overall assistance with your plan, Business Link advisors will also be able to help you out. There is an awful lot of free information available online and through the high street banks, so it shouldn't cost a lot of money to write a plan which covers all the main areas. If writing isn't your strong point, then find someone else to do it for you – the whole point of your plan is to communicate your ideas clearly. The last thing you want is for poor spelling and grammar to get in the way of your brilliant idea.

How long should a business plan be?

The answer to this question is really how long do you need it to be? Bear in mind that while it is good to include your assumptions and back-up information, it is really the financial figures that are key. Try to keep the information brief and to the point wherever possible. It is the figures which need to be detailed rather than the blurb. Think about the person who is reading the plan. If they are really busy (which successful investors often are) they won't have time to plough through a 50-page document. As a general rule, keep the documentation as simple and straightforward as possible.

How should a business plan look?

You don't need to spend a fortune on printing and binding your business plan, but presentation is still important. Print it out on good quality paper and have it bound at a printers with a durable top sheet. If you have a company logo, use that on the front cover. Make sure you have a PDF or Word document version which you can e-mail to people.

How accurate does a business plan have to be?

This is a good question. When you are using your plan to get investment or external people on board, the figures need to be credible and convincing and you need to believe honestly that they are correct. As we mentioned earlier, a plan which includes unrealistically high sales or low costs will instantly look suspicious. If you are saying that you will be selling millions of pounds worth of muffins in year 1 of trading, then you had better have the assumptions in your plan to back that up. Investors won't necessarily take your word for it – they will want hard evidence. Anyway, by writing an unrealistic plan, you are setting yourself up for failure and you will be the biggest loser. On the other hand, everybody knows that even the best-laid business plans of mice and men are likely to go awry. Anything could happen and, where start-up businesses are concerned, it usually does. Write a plan which you believe in 100 per cent, but be aware of the effort that needs to go in to make it a reality and of the fact that things will happen both within and outside of your control which will affect your business's performance.

Note: Remember that you shouldn't think of your plan as something which you have to do to show other people. A good plan can help you to understand more about your business and it pays to review it at least once a year.

3

People

WHEN WE FIRST STARTED OUR BUSINESS, we didn't think very much about having to employ people. Obviously we had salaries factored into our business plan to reflect how the company would grow in the future, but we hadn't really thought through the implications of becoming an employer.

There are over 60 million people living in the United Kingdom, and the vast majority work for a living. So it stands to reason that finding staff and keeping hold of them should be a cinch. Shouldn't it?

When you are starting your business – particularly if you are new to running a commercial enterprise or working in the sector which you have chosen – it is often tempting to see other people as the easy 'quick fix' solution to any problems you face. When we were setting up, we would phone people who were more experienced than we were and ask them lots of questions. This included ringing partners at top accountancy firms and asking them for advice on writing a business plan, through to speaking to venture capitalists about finance, and even contacting people who were running successful online businesses for advice about e-commerce systems. We listened hard to that advice and took it on board. 'People are great!' we would think to ourselves. 'Full of great advice and knowledge!'

Where we went wrong, in terms of recruiting staff, was that we somewhat naively believed that everyone we came across would be equally helpful and knowledgeable . . . including the people we hired.

The very first employee we had was a family friend who had previously done some child-minding for Rebecca. She was young, willing and almost completely inexperienced. Because she was younger than we were, was a good personal friend and had no career plan, she was happy to do whatever we asked. She did telesales, advertising sales, bought the milk, answered the phone and was generally lovely. However, as time went on she felt the need to move on and try new things. She did this in quite spectacular style by deciding to become a pole-dancer. As you very quickly learn when employing people, human beings are full of surprises. Or as the Yorkshire saying goes, 'There's nowt so queer as folk'.

Over a five-year period we have had employees of all shapes and sizes (we say this metaphorically and are not talking about their physiques, which would be illegal!). We had temporary workers, permanent workers, temps who became permanents, perms who became temps, part-timers, full-timers and flexi-timers. We also had contractors, consultants, freelancers and non-executive directors. For our particular business we have had to employ lots of different people to fill lots of different roles. Sales people, marketing people, production people, administration people . . . the list goes on farther than the eye can see. Some of these people have stuck with us through thick and thin. Others bailed out a fortnight after starting. And quite a few went on their way somewhere between these two extremes.

HUMAN RESOURCE PLANNING

When you are putting your business plan together, you should try to get some idea of how many people you will need in order for your business to grow effectively and how much these people will cost. This involves budgeting for obvious things such as wages and salaries, but there are also more incidental costs that need to be considered – things like employers' National Insurance and provision of any benefits you intend giving. You must also remember to include the cost of recruiting staff in the first place. This can include recruitment fees if you are using an agency or the costs of advertising in the media if you do things directly.

It is really important to plan for your people and to draw a chart of your organisation which shows exactly who will be reporting to whom. Every business plan will have commercial objectives which are driven by people, and those commercial objectives need to be turned into specific jobs and job descriptions. You can then use the job descriptions to start the recruitment process. This can take ages. By the time you have done the planning, placed advertisements, collated responses, interviewed potentially suitable candidates and made the job offer, weeks if not months can have passed. Allow for this in your business plan so that, once you have an idea of who you will need to do what and when, you can start the recruitment process.

Helen Straw is an HR consultant who works with businesses of all shapes and sizes. According to her, these are the most common mistakes SMEs make when recruiting:

★ **Not being clear about the job role before starting the recruitment process – a job description and specification will help this.**

★ Forgetting to check out how the salary on offer compares to other similar business sectors and geographical locations – benchmarking can be very useful. Decide in advance how you want to pitch your salary rates compared to any competitors.

★ Advertising in the wrong place and then wondering why you either have no applications or some very strange ones – research the best place to advertise for your type of business.

★ Not specifying the closing date on the advert and receiving applications long after you have found somebody – be specific and stick to it!

★ Not carrying out a thorough selection process – don't be afraid to use different styles of questioning, practical tests, show them around the premises, let them get a feel for what it would be like working for you.

★ Not taking up references – better to know now than to find out something awful at a later stage!

★ Not using a probationary period, which would need to be specified in any offer letter and contract – this way both parties can see if it was the right choice.

★ Not carrying out a thorough induction process when the new employee starts – more people leave employment in the first six months than at any other time.

THE RECRUITMENT PROCESS

It can be hard to know where to start when recruiting for staff. The success you have depends very much on your planning and preparation. Recruitment can be an expensive process, particularly if you end up with the wrong person in the job. One of the most common things that you can get wrong as an employer is to wish people into a particular role. This means that, due to desperation, or sometimes just because you like them, you end up offering someone a job even though you know at the back of your mind that they aren't quite right. Sooner or later this approach will come back to haunt you. Remember that you are not running a job-creation scheme. Rather, your business has occupational requirements that need to be filled by people with the right skills and experience. Fortunately, there are some straightforward things that you can do to make the recruitment process easier and that will automatically increase the chances of you finding a suitable person for any given role.

In our experience (and believe us it's been hard earned), you will have to do some basic preparation and planning before you even start the recruitment process. It took us three years to understand that, without this preparation, we were always going to end up with people leaving or having to get rid of them. Here are some basic steps which you can take to ensure that you stand the best possible chance of recruiting the people that you really need.

WRITE A JOB DESCRIPTION AND A JOB SPECIFICATION

Before you start advertising your position, you need to be 100 per cent clear about what the job is and the type of person you are looking for to do that job. When you are running a small business it can be tempting to recruit someone just because they seem valuable in a vague, almost indefinable sense. This is almost always short-sighted. Human beings generally like clearly-stated expectations and a clearly-defined role. One of the biggest and easiest mistakes to make is to recruit someone without giving them a specific description of what role they will be required to play and exactly what the job entails. When you are running your own company and making your first foray into the world of recruitment, it can be tempting just to get someone in to 'help out'. But you really need to write down all of the things that you need your staff to do, then create specific job titles around those things.

For example, when we were starting out we needed to bring people in to deal with outgoing mail, make telesales calls, write marketing letters, do the bookkeeping and meet and greet visitors. There are at least four jobs there and even a fantastic all-rounder wouldn't have been able to deal with all of them, no matter how well they juggled their responsibilities.

To avoid such pitfalls, you need to write both a job description and a job specification. A job description is about the job. A good one will help any potential candidate reading it to understand exactly what the job involves and should include each of the following elements:

★ The *specific* title of the job offered. For example, 'Personal Assistant to the Managing Director', as opposed to simply 'PA'.
★ A brief description of what your business does.
★ Whether the job is temporary or permanent, full or part time.
★ What the purpose of the job is – how does it fit into the picture of the company as a whole?
★ Who the person in that role will be reporting to.

★ Who the person in that role will be responsible for.
★ What the person in that role will be responsible for doing (you can break this down into tasks and responsibilities, but you don't need to go into minute detail).
★ Typical working hours per week.
★ Where the post is based (i.e. in the office or in the field, as well as the geographical location).
★ What the pay scale is.

A job specification is related to the applicant. It tells potential candidates exactly what skills and experience you need them to have before they apply for the job. A job specification should cover the following points:

★ The specific title of the job offered.
★ Who the person in that role will be reporting to.
★ What the purpose of the job is.

When you have covered these things, write down what you regard as being essential attributes for the applicant to possess, and then those that are desirable.

For example, out of the following list, there will be some attributes that you identify as essential, and some which will be desirable:

★ experience
★ skills
★ knowledge
★ qualifications
★ background
★ other

Once you have written down exactly what you are looking for, it will help you to understand who you need to fill the job. Then, when you start receiving CVs and applications, you can use your job specification to filter out those applications from candidates who don't meet your criteria.

WHERE TO FIND STAFF

There are eight main ways of finding staff, which we will discuss in turn. Regardless of the method used, you need to be clear about your timescales, so put a deadline for responses on your advertisement or when speaking to an agency.

1 Use the job centre

Advertising a vacancy in a job centre is very much like taking a pin and sticking it at random in the phone book. It has a glorious 'roll the dice' feel to it, as if you are gambling on finding someone good. We have found one or two great people through the job centre, but it has to be said that they were the rare jackpot finds. In most cases, we would get phone calls in response to the advertisement and book candidates in for interviews, but we would never hear from them again. On more than one occasion we have had someone in for interviews, offered them a job which they have accepted, only to find that they don't turn up to start work. They mysteriously become impossible to contact and that's the last you hear of them.

To be honest, this kind of thing makes you wonder if some people just go to interviews for something to do. Maybe it gives them the chance to dress up, get out for the day and meet new people. Perhaps it makes a change from a repetitive diet of daytime television. Or maybe they are just too nervous to say that actually they don't like the look of you and wouldn't be employed by your company if you offered them a million pounds. As we said earlier, there's nowt so queer as folk.

Despite all of this, the job centre is always worth a go, particularly for the lower end of the pay scale roles. However, putting an advert up for a managing director would probably be wishful thinking . . . although we suppose that it would make for an interesting social experiment.

2 Use local colleges and universities

If the role you are looking to fill is suitable for college leavers or graduates, then most higher education institutions have notice boards, websites, e-mail bulletins and career services which offer a very cost-effective way of tapping into a pool of fresh talent.

The downside of this approach is that many graduates will be suffering from 'post-graduation blind panic' syndrome, and this can lead to them applying for jobs for which they are patently unsuited. Or they may be going through a huge upheaval period when they are faced with lots of big decisions, don't know where they want to live, what they want to do, or how they are going to repay their student debts. In both cases, these factors can lead to you employing a promising individual who initially seems perfectly suited to the position, but who begins to question their decision after a few months and suddenly chooses to go backpacking in Nepal or train as an accountant instead.

In our experience, this kind of thing is quite common when recruiting people straight out of university, but there are still enough exceptions to the rule to make this approach worth considering.

3 Advertise in local or national press

Unless the job you are advertising or the sector you work in is very specific, advertising your vacancy in the press can be a bit of a long shot. Specific jobs are the easiest – for example, if you wanted to hire a teacher, you would find that potential teachers often turn to the *Times Educational Supplement* for job advertisements. Or if you wanted someone in publishing, you would probably get good results by advertising in the media section of the *Guardian*. Because placement of your advertisement is so important, you should think very carefully about the demographics of the people who read a particular publication and ask yourself if that readership is likely to match your requirements.

Writing an advertisement for a publication isn't as straightforward as most people tend to assume. It has to be eye catching (especially if you can't afford a large ad space) as well as informative. The basic information which needs to be provided in the text of your advertisement includes:

* the specific title of the job offered
* the main responsibilities involved
* what kind of company you are
* your contact details
* salary or package details (this is optional)
* any other appealing factors about the position
* the deadline for applications

Remember that your job will need to stand out from the crowd, so think carefully about ways to make your opportunity look more appealing than others on the page. Maybe you could use a fancy border for the advert, or a particularly bold headline. Look at the approach taken by other advertisers in the same publication and then strive to be different. Originality in advertising, as in business itself, often goes a long way.

When booking advertising space in the press, you should be prepared to haggle for the best possible price and also for the best position on the page. The eye is naturally drawn to the bottom or centre right of a double-page spread, so those are the areas to aim for if at all possible.

There are various equal opportunity laws in place which make it illegal to discriminate against candidates because of their race, sex, disability, sexual orientation or religion. You could add a line to your advert stating that you are an equal opportunities employer, just to state the obvious. If you are unsure about what you can or can't write in a job advertisement, or about equal opportunities in general, contact ACAS on 08457 47 47 47 or take a look at its website at **www.acas.org.uk**.

4 Use word of mouth

Sometimes you just happen to hear about the right person at the right time, or they hear about your opportunity and come to you directly. Word of mouth is very important across all kind of industries and at all levels of organisation. If you can find one person who is well connected in your sector, he or she will often know people – either directly or indirectly – who are currently looking for your kind of work, or are about to move on and will be looking for your kind of work in the near future. We have recruited a number of our more senior and experienced staff in this way. Never take recommendations on face value though – always check out the candidate, no matter who suggested them.

5 Use recruitment agencies

Recruitment agents are to the 21st century what estate agents were to the 20th century. They are working in a boom market, where demand exceeds supply, and have garnered a poor reputation for themselves as a result. When recruiting through an agent, you need to be absolutely sure that you have made the job specification and description clear to that agent. For example, if your job specification states that the candidate needs to have at least three years' experience in a related field and they keep sending you details of people who have just left university, you need to explain your needs to them again – but perhaps even more slowly this time. If they persist in sending you unsuitable candidates and wasting your time with irrelevant CVs, then find another agency. There are a lot of them out there and some are better than others.

Beware of recruitment agent speak. They are selling people to you in much the same way that estate agents sell houses. They may say 'this candidate is the perfect fit for your business' – but then an estate agent will sell a shed as 'a compact living space with incredible potential'. In short, believe it when you see it.

Always make sure that you understand the terms of the agent you deal with. When you take a candidate on as a temporary worker, there are many benefits to you, including the facts that they are actually employed by the agency rather than you and that you can get rid of them very quickly if they don't work out. Of course, if you want to keep them working with you on a permanent basis, you will need to pay an agency fee for the privilege. As with all things, this fee is negotiable and you should haggle for a deal that you are happy with.

6 Use headhunters

Headhunters operate in a similar way to recruitment agents, in that they work on behalf of the employer to find staff and receive a commission when they are successful. Headhunters generally work at a much higher level than agencies and tend to be well-connected individuals who specialise in particular sectors. They are expensive, but are definitely an option when you are looking for senior management positions or recruiting at director level.

To work effectively with a headhunter you need to know exactly what you are looking for, how much you are willing to spend on finding the employee you need, and what the job consists of. If there are any grey areas, the whole exercise will quickly prove to be expensive and ineffectual.

7 Consider 'on spec' CVs

Once your company gets in the phonebook, has a website and begins enjoying some level of public awareness, you may find that you start to receive CVs from people who are interested in working for you. How many CVs you get depends on the kind of business that you run. As a youth-orientated publishing business, we do get quite a few applicants in this way. It obviously depends on whether you have a vacancy available as to whether you contact the person and invite them for interview, but usually if someone has made the effort to research your business and write to you they are worth at least keeping on file.

It is a good idea to have a straightforward procedure in place for dealing with CVs that are sent to you in this way. First, respond to the applicant with a standard letter saying 'thank you for contacting us'. If you want them to come in for an interview, ask them to do so. If you don't want to pursue an interview at this point but may decide to do so later, let them know in the letter that you will retain their CV on file for a 12-month period and will contact them if a suitable position arises. Of course, you should file CVs received in this way in a safe place. Under the Data Protection Act you should retain this information for a defined period, then destroy it.

8 Use the Internet

Recruitment websites are many and varied. How successful you will be in finding the right person depends on the kind of person you are looking for. For instance, if the job vacancy that you want to fill is very specific or technical, you may be better off advertising through specialist online websites rather than generic recruitment sites. When looking for people in this way, make sure you are clear about the location of the job and the duration of the contract to prevent any confusion.

Dealing with responses

It begins as soon as you receive the CVs. Some CVs will be slick and impressive, full of slippery words that gloss over things like sudden departures from previous positions or gaps between jobs that don't quite ring true. Other CVs will be so rudimentary that you will wonder exactly what the person has done with themselves since leaving school. Some will proudly declare sexual orientation along with gender ('female but happy to swing both ways, especially after a few Breezers'). Others will provide endless lists of hobbies and pastimes (in our opinion people with hobbies clearly have too much time on their hands, but that's purely a bitter personal view). Jokey CVs will want to be your best friend. Others will bang on about being a 'goals-oriented team player with proven results' – whatever that means.

At the end of the day, a CV should be an accurate reflection of the skills and experiences of an individual. Unfortunately (as you will eventually discover yourself), this is not always the case and you should never jump to conclusions about someone's suitability for the job based on their CV alone.

When you are looking at a CV, check the details against your job specification. Does it show evidence of those things listed on your job spec as being 'necessary' or 'desirable'? If not, the best response is to drop the applicant a quick letter saying, 'Thank you for taking the trouble to send in your CV. Unfortunately, we will not be taking your application further on this occasion . . .'

A good idea which can save time and mental energy is to set up some kind of simple scoring mechanism to help you process and grade CVs received from applicants. If you have five things listed on your job spec as being necessary attributes, simply give one point for every relevant point on the CV. A great applicant will score four or five out of five. A poor one will score one or two, but the CV might still be worth holding on file for an alternative position in the future.

The next step is to draw up a list of applicants who score highly (and, to some extent, those who you are most interested in). You then need to contact these people and invite them to attend an interview. You can do this in writing, by e-mail or by phone – it can be a good idea just to give them a ring and have an informal chat on the phone to get a feel for them on a more personal level.

For some jobs, an application form process may be more useful. We have never had to use one, as we don't have enough similar roles in our organisation to make a standard form very useful, but application forms are better than CVs for making straightforward like-for-like comparisons between interested candidates.

CONDUCTING INTERVIEWS

Interviewing candidates can often seem like a very time-consuming exercise (especially when you're particularly busy running the business), but it is nevertheless an essential one. The good news is that if you have a clear job description and job specification in place, have advertised the job accurately, have sorted through applications and CVs according to your job spec and have then drawn up a shortlist, you should have filtered out almost all of the time wasters and 'unsuitables'.

Although it sounds obvious, your first priority must be to make sure that the candidates are clear about when the interview is, where it is being held and at what time. Ideally, all of this information should be presented in a letter inviting the applicant to attend the interview.

When this matter has been taken care of, your next priority should be to establish exactly what information you want to gain from the interview. Instead of interviewing by the seat of your pants, you need to make sure that the interview has a clear structure and that you have planned out your questions in advance. If you are interviewing more than one person for a job, it is really important to ask the same questions at each interview, as this will allow you to make true and fair comparisons between candidates.

Ideally, you should have a second person present at the interview to take notes and give you a second opinion. Different people pick up on different things, and having someone else assessing a candidate at the same time will help you to build a much better picture of the applicant and thereby reduce the chance of you making a wrong decision.

Before you go into an interview with a candidate, you should make sure that you have read their CV or application form thoroughly and have made notes of any areas which need further exploration. On a more prosaic level, make sure that you have turned off the phone and won't be disturbed when the interviewing takes place.

Questions to ask in interviews:
★ What experience do you have which is relevant to this position?
★ What do you see as your specific strengths and weaknesses?
★ What are your goals for your career?
★ What do you like most about your current job?
★ What do you dislike about it?

Questions not to ask in interviews:
★ Are you planning on starting a family soon/having more kids?
★ Does your religion mean that you will need extra time off at holiday periods?
★ Does your disability mean that you will need time off for hospital visits?
★ Are you responsible for taking care of any elderly relatives?

In short, avoid asking anything personal which could get you into trouble under the following Acts of Parliament:

★ Sex Discrimination Act 1975
★ Race Relations Act 1976
★ Disability Discrimination Act 1995
★ New age discrimination law coming in October 2006

And people wonder why small businesses are reluctant to employ staff!

Seriously though, much of this red tape is just good common sense. And if you need someone good, you'll employ them for their brains and their ability, not for their skin colour or gender.

After the interview

The idea of a first interview is to give you some background about each candidate and what makes them tick, after which you should be able to draw up a further shortlist of candidates who you may like to see for a second interview. The purpose of the second interview is to decide which of the short-listed candidates would be best for the job.

In the second interview you can go into more detail. You can set tests, go through role plays and team exercises or use any other procedure which you think is necessary to find the right person. If you are carrying out tests, you'll need to have a procedure or a policy in place for feeding results back to the applicants if they ask for them. And, of course, the results of such tests will need to be kept in a way that complies with the Data Protection Act.

The second interview also provides a good chance for you to get to know the applicant a little better. Ask him or her to give examples of when they felt most challenged by their work or how they cope with being under pressure, or to give examples of times when they have worked particularly well on their own initiative. The questions you ask here will be determined by the nature of the vacancy applied for and the kind of business you are running.

In all interviews, you should keep the needs of your business constantly in mind and try to keep your personal feelings out of the equation. It could be that the applicant you like the most may not be the best person for the job. One of the key issues that we have found when recruiting staff is that we inevitably end up being drawn to people who are actually a bit like us. So at one point we had a company that was almost entirely made up of creative and projects people, rather than what we really needed, which were sales and commercial people. The single most effective way of avoiding this common pitfall is always to recruit using a strong job description and job specification, and then marking applications and CVs accordingly.

THE JOB OFFER

Hopefully, after all this effort, you will emerge with an ideal candidate. He or she will have submitted a strong CV which demonstrates lots of skills and experience, backed up with evidence at the interview stage. This being the case, you can now make a job offer, subject to references.

It is always worth pursuing references. If someone can't supply you with two previous employers as referees then the alarm bells should start ringing immediately. The first and last time we employed someone without checking references was when we recruited for a role and got an apparently strong candidate who was able to start immediately. I can't remember why on earth we didn't check out both of his referees, but we didn't. Two weeks after he had started with us he suddenly went off sick, though we were fairly certain that the sickness wasn't genuine. We looked at what this individual had been doing since starting and it was obvious that it was anything but what we needed him to do. When we tried to fire him it turned out that the candidate had previously trained as a solicitor and still had contacts at a big city law firm, as we got a stern letter from his solicitor shortly afterwards informing us that his client would be taking us to a tribunal for unlawful deduction of wages. We then thought to contact his previous employer, who informed us that he had had to get rid of the candidate as being 'incompatible with the company'. Now there are many reasons why perfectly good people are fired, but there was obviously something wrong here and it would certainly have made us think twice about employing the candidate had we checked him out properly.

To make a formal job offer, you need a letter which is dated and signed by a director (i.e. you). This letter needs to state the job title, the starting salary, the start date, the basis of employment (full time, part time, permanent or temporary; any probationary period) and where the position will be based. If the job comes with any other benefits, such as a car allowance or bonuses and/or commission, these also need to be detailed.

Problem solved!

So, there you have it – one new member of staff and one less thing to worry about. Or so you would hope. In reality, this is where the real hard work starts.

In our experience, coming up with ideas and driving the business forward is the easy bit. The difficult thing is finding, managing, developing and retaining good people. Part of the problem with small businesses is that things tend to change fairly frequently. One product doesn't work, so you do something else. One marketing technique isn't working, so you amend it. This is one of the great things about being a small company – you have the freedom and ability to respond to circumstances.

However, not everybody likes change. In fact, many people are actually quite hostile to change and will do pretty much anything to prevent it. So, as an entrepreneur, you might think that it would be a fabulous idea to create a new product in response to a new government initiative for schools (that way the cash lies, and besides, new products are much more interesting than existing ones). But your decisions will impact on the daily working life of your staff. If you aren't completely clear with them about why you are making these decisions and why they are having to drop something they are used to and venture into what may be unknown territory, they will often react badly. So if you are running a business that does change direction frequently, make sure you tell people that this is your culture when you are recruiting. Ask them to give you examples of when they have previously had to adapt to change in the working life. In other words, prepare them for what is likely to be ahead.

Once you've got your member of staff, you will need to give him or her some kind of induction. You can't expect people to pick things up as quickly as you can perhaps, or to take on new tasks with relish. Anyway, you want to make sure that they know what they are doing, and that *you* know what they are doing. A typical induction will take place over the course of a day to two weeks. It can be a good idea to have a list of things to run through on day one and a schedule for what they will need to get their heads around over an initial, clearly defined period.

At a very basic level, an induction period should include:

★ **Introductions to other members of staff and their responsibilities.**

★ **Building security arrangements. For example, will the new person need to know an alarm code to get into the** building? Or will they need their own set of keys? (You may want to get them settled in before you give them these.)

★ Health and safety procedures. This includes the identification of fire exits and an explanation of first aid procedures and how to deal with any hazardous activities that are present in the job or in the associated environment.

★ Office rules. Here the employee needs to be told how long he or she can expect at break and lunch times, the company rules relating to Internet and e-mail usage, dress codes, appropriate ways of answering the telephone, the company policy concerning smokers and so on.

★ Basic IT training, so that the employee can use the company computers and intranet, access databases, understand the networks in place and use the telephone system.

A separate part of the induction process should relate to any specific training or information that the employee will need in order to carry out his or her specific role-related tasks. This is obviously down to you to plan and implement, and to monitor their progress.

It is always a good idea to record your induction processes and tick boxes when things are completed. Then get the employee to sign and date this record when the induction process is finished, before putting the document into the employee file.

PERSONNEL FILES

When you employ people, you naturally tend to think about starting new relationships (of a business nature, of course!). Or you think about starting a new phase of your business development. Or starting a new team. This is all true, but what you are also doing is starting an avalanche of paperwork and *filing*.

We are often asked if red tape and bureaucracy have prevented our business from developing to its full extent. In terms of tax and company law, the answer is no; that hasn't been the case in our experience. But if we are talking about employment law, then that is another story. Our personnel files are daily reminders of the extent to which employment law has imposed itself on the running of a small business, and the bottom line is that you can't operate legally without keeping your paperwork in order.

For every person you employ, you should create a file in which the following documents need to be kept:

★ the job description
★ the job specification
★ a copy of the job advertisement the employee responded to
★ the employee's CV
★ a copy of the invitation to interview
★ the interview notes
★ your offer letter
★ any formal acceptance letter from the employee
★ their P45
★ their references
★ a copy of their passport or driving licence to prove their legal right to work in the UK under the Asylum and Immigration Act (if the job requires them to drive it is

always worth taking a copy of their driving licence anyway, in order to have proof on file that it is clean and valid)

★ contact details in case of emergency
★ home and mobile telephone contact details
★ documents relating to commission sheets or bonuses, signed and agreed by all parties
★ dates for performance reviews. As time goes on you will also need to put notes from these reviews into the file
★ any disciplinary notes
★ and finally, the biggie – their employment contract

All of this may seem a bit over the top – especially if you are only employing part-time or junior staff. But every employee has very strong rights according to the law, and having all of this documentation in place just gives you as an employer a bit of security and clarity if, for any reason, it all goes horribly wrong. Small businesses slip up in employment law all the time simply because proper written records haven't been kept of their employee's contract, disciplinary record or review meetings. Better safe than sorry!

CONTRACTS OF EMPLOYMENT

Of course your legal protection as an employer is only as strong as the contracts you have in place with your staff. It is definitely worth asking a solicitor or Business Link advisor for help in sourcing and developing a good contract of employment for your employees, but as a bare minimum you should make sure that your contracts include the following details:

★ **The job title.** For example, 'The Company will employ the Employee as Marketing Manager.' Try to be as specific as possible so that you can avoid future disagreements over what role the employee is expected to play.

★ **Employment duties.** This section should outline the duties and responsibilities of the position. You don't need to be absolutely exhaustive here (there's no need to itemise everything that you want a cleaning lady to polish), but you do need to detail the main categories of responsibility to avoid misunderstanding.

★ **Terms of employment.** Will the employee be working for you for a limited period, such as 12 or 18 months? Or will the employment be ongoing until the contract of employment is terminated by either party? You need to make this clear in this section, specifying start and – if necessary – end dates.

★ **Termination.** This section should explain how the contract may be terminated by either party, giving details of the notice period required and the form in which notice must be given (in almost all cases, written notice is preferable to verbal).

★ **Salary details.** How much will the employee be paid and how often? If commission payments and/or bonuses will be paid, these also need to be outlined.

★ **Pension and benefits.** If your employee will qualify for a company pension scheme, a company car or any other benefits, you should say so here.

★ **Sickness benefits.** How will your employee be paid during periods of sickness? What kind of proof will be required of sickness (medical certificates etc).

★ **Expenses.** Will your company pay business expenses on behalf of the employee? If so, you should outline the procedure here.

★ **Confidentiality.** It is always a good idea to state in the contract of employment that the personal details of the employee will be kept confidential at all times.

There are other sections which can also be included in a contract of employment, depending on the specific nature of your business, but these are the main areas that tend to apply across the board.

MANAGING STAFF

Unless you have managed people before, this is one of the key things that you will be least prepared for when starting a new business. We would by no means claim to be the world's best people managers. But since we've been there, done that and already gone through the often difficult process of learning by experience, you might benefit a little from some of the lessons we have learned (even though the learning process never really ends and we are still making progress in this area). Here then are some basic rules of management which you may find useful in getting your staff to respect you and work more effectively for you:

Rule number 1: Always tell it exactly how it is. Running a business makes you realise how – in normal everyday life and particularly when you are working for a bigger organisation – you very rarely have to state the obvious. It's not that we weave a web of lies in our daily intercourse with others, but it is human nature to want to avoid confrontation and conflict. Because of this, very often in business you will be faced with a choice: should you tell your staff what you think they want to hear, or do you tell them the truth, even if this might be more awkward for you and harder for them to take?

While it is tempting to avoid the issue and any potential confrontation, in the long term such evasion does not pay off. Communication is at the heart of any relationship and you need to have the courage of your convictions when you are running your own business.

Rule number 2: Don't put off the things you least want to do. It is usually these very things that are most important when it comes to managing people. If someone needs a warning about their work or behaviour, then issue that warning straight away. If you are unhappy about a working relationship, tell the other person immediately. If you think someone has done a brilliant job, then let them know straight away.

Rule number 3: Be open about your planning and your decision-making. Keeping people informed will keep people on your side. Nobody really like surprises, especially when it comes to their working lives. Besides, asking other people for their opinion can often be useful. However, always bear rule number 4 in mind:

Rule number 4: Don't listen to too many other people. Or, to put it more elegantly, listen to them but let your own gut instinct guide you when it comes to making a final decision. Having the input of others is useful from an information-gathering point of view, but you can't effectively run any business by committee.

We love speaking to women who successfully manage large companies. It is a source of inspiration to us, and it is always worth talking to other people who are successfully managing staff and growing a team to learn from them.

JULIE KENNY, MANAGING DIRECTOR OF PYRONIX LTD

We usually recruit through adverts in the local press and in the job centre, and our staff are trained on the job. There were loads of mistakes made while we were expanding so quickly and too many recruitment decisions taken on the basis of a quick interview and a piece of paper. You learn, though, that better choices and decisions are made if you have clear values and a vision.

You need to have what I call 'Pyronix values' to work here. I do the induction course myself and tell employees about the company and why they are as important as me in the grand scheme of things. Employees do tend to follow the leader. We have been known to create job roles for good people, because you have to be more creative when you are recruiting for a growing business. When it comes to bad people, I've tried to work with people and change people, but bad apples will taint others.

You have to accept that some people come to work because they have to work, not because they love it. I used to think that if I treated people right, nobody would leave, but this just isn't the case. What I've learned is that you can't pussyfoot around people. You create mutual respect by tackling issues straight on. Having said that, I had three weeks of sleepless nights when I first had to sack someone, but you have to take a deep breath and do it for the sake of the business.

In 1998 we created a staff consultative committee at Pyronix and we still use it to talk about staff issues. Communication is so important – I send all my staff birthday cards and Christmas cards. I love my staff. I don't think of myself as the boss – they are like family to me.

Visit Pyronix online at: www.pyronix.com

JULIA MIDDLETON, FOUNDER AND CEO OF COMMON PURPOSE

I let strategy come out of people, not people out of strategy. You contort the strategy to attract, develop and suit the talented. Also, you need to communicate a sense of purpose. So you bore yourself to tears, as a chief executive, repeating the vision all the time. If you're a successful chief executive, by the end of every week you will have repeated the vision so many times that everybody will be going barking. The time when you really screw up is usually when you've forgotten to repeat the vision enough.

It took me too long to impose my management style on the organisation. Gerry Robinson, chairman of the Arts Council, was very helpful. He encouraged me to say, 'There are five different ways of running this business. All five are highly credible. I'm running it though, so we're going to do it my way.'

Gerry made me realise that by saying I want to run things

this way didn't mean the others were wrong. I wish I'd realised that earlier.

Visit Common Purpose online at:
www.commonpurpose.org.uk

UNDERSTANDING YOURSELF AND YOUR ROLE AS A LEADER

Running your own business involves a steep learning curve in many respects, but perhaps the one thing that you will learn the most about is your own strengths and weaknesses. Having an understanding of your own skills and personality is the best possible starting point for understanding other people. Without a little self-awareness, it is very hard to manage others. On a practical level, self-awareness is handy when you are building your team. Understand where your weak points are and you can find people to help support the business in those areas. On a more strategic level, you need to understand your own personality so that, when you are faced with a difficult situation, you are aware of your likely reaction to it and can decide whether or not this reaction is appropriate.

Sometimes you have to be brutally honest with yourself about the way you handle other people. If things aren't going to plan, the buck will most likely stop with you – after all, you are the boss. If you can't shoulder that responsibility, then running a business probably isn't for you. Even if you end up with the worst employee in the world who does a terrible job, ultimately it is up to you to spot the problem and sort it out. And if you don't sort it out then, frankly, it's your fault.

Starting a business means embarking on a voyage of self-discovery like no other – you have built a boat from your own ideas, and you have brought money and other people on board. It is now your responsibility to develop the skills to steer this boat through storms and calm waters.

Very few people are naturally good leaders; everyone can do with some training or support. Learning and development and self-discovery are all the brilliant things about business that you never hear about at school, university or in the papers. Business is portrayed as this big cut-throat, sink-or-swim corporate dog fight, when actually it is a massive opportunity for learning – learning about others, learning about economics, learning about commerce, learning about customers, learning about leadership and learning about yourself.

Learn about leadership from heroes. It's important to have heroes or role models when you are starting your own business. Think of people who you admire for what they have achieved. Who do you think handles other people well? How do they communicate? What are their attributes and what can you learn from that? Heroes can come from any background. It isn't necessarily the case that business leaders are automatically most relevant. Rebecca's rather random list of personal heroes includes Ernest Shackleton, Percy Bysshe Shelley and Madonna. Kirsty's heroes are probably horse-orientated. We both think that Steve Jobs of Apple is pretty cool. Don't get hung up on trying to find a business person to emulate. Leaders can be found in lots of different arenas.

If you have a good understanding of your own capabilities and personality traits, you will be able to develop the skills that you need to run your business and manage people more effectively. Sometimes, however, a realistic assessment of your own abilities may lead you to the conclusion that you are really not cut out to manage a team of people. Many entrepreneurs do not make good managers. They tend to be ideas people, or money people, rather than people people. If this is the case, then you need to look at your role in the organisation and how you can move the business forward while having someone else manage the team. This is not easy (if it's difficult to find good employees in general, then good managers are like gold dust), but it is by no means impossible.

RETAINING YOUR STAFF

The single most important thing you can do to ensure good staff retention is to find the right person for the job in the first place and to be 100 per cent clear on what the job involves. Beyond that, there are lots of things that you can do on an ongoing basis that will make your staff want to stick around. These include:

★ Making the working environment a good place to be. Don't panic – this could just mean having decent tea-making facilities and clean toilets rather than installing pool tables and a staff canteen.
★ Organising regular social events – even if it is just going to the pub once a month.
★ Having regular team meetings where people can make their voices heard and let others know what they are doing.
★ Paying people fairly and on time.
★ Giving people contracts which they understand and accept.
★ Having a suggestions box – and actually reading the suggestions that are made.
★ Letting the team know what the management are thinking . . . and making sure that the management know what you are thinking.

★ Having a noticeboard where people can pin information about forthcoming social events and team news.

★ Rewarding and praising employees for achievement in a consistent way.

★ Sorting out problems promptly and having a transparent grievance procedure in place.

★ Being supportive of people.

★ Being relentlessly positive and upbeat, even when you are exhausted and can barely muster the energy to say good morning. If you are down and you show it, you will bring the team down with you. Low morale can quickly become endemic, especially in a relatively small organisation.

★ Having good flexible working, maternity and paternity leave policies.

★ Having regular performance and pay reviews.

No matter how hard you work to make your employees happy, you should always bear in mind that, in small businesses at least, people do tend to come and go. For this reason, if you do have someone with you for three years before they choose to move on, you've had a pretty good innings and anything more than that is a bonus.

GET THE BASICS: MATERNITY AND PATERNITY LEAVE
Maternity leave

Some people think that maternity leave is something that women are entitled to only after a lengthy period of service with a company. This is not the case. All pregnant women are entitled to a number of specific benefits related to maternity. These include:

★ Time off (paid) for visits to the hospital, check-ups and so on.
★ Entitlement to the usual sickness benefits for periods of absence caused by sickness related to pregnancy.
★ A minimum of 26 weeks' maternity leave.
★ All regular benefits of employment (for example, holiday leave etc)
★ The legal right to return to their work after maternity leave has been taken.

Mothers who have been employed for a minimum of 26 weeks by the time they reach the 15th week before their expected week of childbirth are also entitled to:

★ Up to 26 weeks' additional maternity leave. This makes it possible for a woman to have one year of maternity leave in total. However, the additional 26 weeks of leave is unpaid.
★ The legal right to return to their job after maternity leave has been taken, or to a similar job at a similar level if this is not possible due to the nature of the business.

Paternity leave

Whereas all pregnant women are entitled to at least 26 weeks of maternity leave regardless of how long they have been working with you, paternity leave is only a legal entitlement for men who have been employed for a minimum of 26 weeks by the time they reach the 15th week before their partner's expected week of childbirth.

The current paternity leave entitlement in the United Kingdom is two weeks of leave which can be taken 'at or around' the date of the child's birth. The flexibility here is sensible, as it allows the father to take his two weeks at a time which will be of most use to his partner and child. However, because this flexibility gives fathers an option over exactly when they take their leave, men are required to give you 28 days' notice of when they want their Statutory Paternity Pay to start.

Note: The cost of maternity and paternity pay is borne by the taxpayer, rather than the business, so don't panic – your business won't be paying someone who isn't working, you can claim it back from HM Revenue & Customs. For more information, visit **www.hmrc.gov.uk**.

MANAGING THE PERFORMANCE OF STAFF

Once you have people working for you, you need to ensure that they are doing their jobs properly and that they are happy with what they are doing. To do this you should review their progress regularly. This can be done informally in regular meetings, during which you can check that their work is satisfactory and that they aren't struggling with their tasks. Then you can have more formal, less frequent performance review meetings which need to be monitored. A typical performance review should be:

★ **Planned.** Before the review, be clear about what areas of performance you wish to discuss and have an equally clear way of measuring these areas. Unless you can actually measure current performance (and therefore compare it to past performance) then reviews won't be as useful as they could be.

★ **Relevant.** The review should focus on areas of

125

performance which are directly relevant to the official role and responsibilities of the employee. For example, if you are reviewing the performance of a sales rep, focus on things like sales targets and customer referrals. Don't waste time on minor peripheral duties.

★ **Co-operative.** The review should not be set up so that it suggests an 'employer versus employee' scenario, as this is too confrontational. Instead, it should be viewed as an opportunity for both you and the employee to work together and find ways of improving performance and formally recognising good work that has already been done.

★ **Scheduled.** No employee likes being 'ambushed' with a surprise review, so schedule them and let your employees know when they will take place. A side benefit of scheduling reviews is that employees will automatically begin to monitor – and improve – their own performance in the meantime.

★ **Action-oriented.** A 60-minute moan (or hug fest) won't do your business an ounce of good. Give praise where it is due, but make your reviews action-oriented by setting goals with your employee which they agree to pursue as a way of improving their performance.

★ **Recorded.** To ensure that both you and your employee are clear on what has been said and agreed, keep notes of all your reviews (and the actions that have been set) and get the employee to read, sign and date them. Then file these notes in your employee's file so that they can be referred to in the future.

You can track performance reviews against key performance indicators or 'KPIs'. A KPI is something that you have written and agreed with the employee in advance and helps you to track their progress. For example, if a sales person is due to sell 50 cakes by the end of the year, a KPI they would have for June would be to have sold 25 cakes. If they haven't sold that many cakes then you need to know why. If they have hit their KPI or exceeded it, then praise and recognition are due. This is a very simplistic example, but KPIs do work for all roles. They should be linked to the job description, which in turn should be linked to the company plan. Basically, whatever your business plan is telling you needs to be achieved, should be translated into a job description, which is then distilled down into KPIs. If KPIs are hit or exceeded at the end of the financial year, then that person has fulfilled their job description, and that part of the business plan will have been achieved. Everyone is happy!

IF YOU NEED TO GET RID OF SOMEONE

People leave employment for all sorts of reasons. Sometimes they are made redundant when the business no longer needs that role to be filled. Sometimes they have had enough, or just want to move on, and so they resign. And occasionally they get fired.

There is no nice way of firing someone, even if they are a useless employee and you are glad to see the back of them. As Julie Kenny said (page 119), you just have to take a deep breath, look them in the eye and tell them that they are no longer needed. However, because of employment law, it is increasingly difficult to fire people. This is why it is so important to recruit the right person for the right job in the first place. Hiring the wrong person can prove to be an expensive mistake.

Generally speaking, if you have an issue with an employee and their performance or behaviour, and if they have been employed by you for more than a year, you need to follow a disciplinary procedure if you want to fire them without any legal repercussions. There are certain things which count as gross misconduct, which mean that you can fire them on the spot, but these are fairly limited and include serious misdemeanours such as stealing from the company or harassing other employees.

A fairly standard disciplinary procedure would consist of the following steps:

★ **An informal verbal warning.** This would be appropriate for a relatively minor offence, such as routinely failing to keep a room tidy (which might have health and safety implications).

★ **A formal verbal warning.** This would be given for more serious offences, or for minor offences where previous informal warnings have not been heeded.

★ **A written warning.** This is an official letter and is usually reserved for even more serious offences (though not ones which qualify for dismissal), or for offences where previous formal verbal warnings have not been heeded. A copy of this written warning should be kept in the employee's file.

★ **A final written warning.** If the previous written warning isn't effective, this final written warning should state that repetition of the offence will result in dismissal.

All of these will need to be recorded and put in the relevant employee's personnel file for your reference. It is important that you have a standard disciplinary procedure in writing and that your employees are fully aware of what this procedure involves. Under most circumstances (and assuming that you have hired good people, as discussed earlier), you will rarely have to give written warnings, let alone a final written warning. But once in a while someone will do something repeatedly that demands you take a tough stance, and it's on these occasions that a standard disciplinary procedure will come in handy.

In cases where instant dismissal is warranted (which means that the employee is guilty of gross misconduct) then you still have to follow certain steps for the dismissal to be legal. These steps are:

★ Issue a written statement which details the actions and/ or behaviour which has led to the dismissal and tells the employee that they have a right to appeal against your decision.

★ Hold an appeal meeting where the gross misconduct is discussed and the decision reviewed objectively. In most cases the decision to dismiss will stand, but in some cases you will decide to uphold the appeal and reinstate the employee.

We'll be perfectly frank here – the laws concerning staff discipline and dismissal are an absolute minefield, and no matter how long we spend outlining our take on the subject, you will still need to do your own homework so that you are aware of the latest rules and regulations. For further details on this fascinating (though somewhat depressing) subject, visit the dismissal section of the Business Link website, which can be found at **www.businesslink.gov.uk**, or read up on it at **www.acas.org.uk**.

TO SUM UP . . .

★ Don't expect employees to solve your problems for you.
★ Draw up a list of business objectives (preferably taken from your business plan) and work out how these translate into job descriptions and job specifications.
★ Interview candidates according to the job description and job specification, not according to whether or not you like them.
★ Keep on top of your personnel files.
★ Develop your own skills as a leader.
★ Have heroes who inspire you to lead.
★ Get as much help as you can with employment law issues before you employ anyone.

4

Finding Premises

ONE OF THE MAIN THINGS TO think about when starting your own business is where you will operate from. In other words, do you want or need to find premises? Different businesses will obviously have different needs in this respect, but many start-ups do find this to be one of the most difficult hurdles to overcome.

The reason for this is because commercial landlords invariably want their tenants to sign very long-term leases. This secures their income and means that they don't have to keep paying solicitors to draw up new contracts or rental agreements. However, if you are a start-up owner/manager, long-term leases are the last thing that you want. When you are starting your own business, signing up for a ten-year lease just seems (and is!) unrealistic. This is a completely new venture and making any long-term commitment financially or legally is a big risk to take. We'll look at that aspect of starting up a little later, but first let's discuss some of the basic questions that you should ask yourself when considering taking out a lease on business premises:

★ **Do you actually have to rent premises in the first place?**

Working from home is always a cheaper option and can often make it easier to combine business operations with childcare or family responsibilities. Also, if your work involves going out to see clients and customers rather than them coming to see you, you may not need to rent office space.

★ If you are starting a business which will rely on passing trade, or you need to rent shop premises, it is vital that you get the location right. Is the area you are looking at suitable for your venture? Will clients or customers find it accessible? What other shops are in the vicinity? In business you will always face competition, but you don't want to make life more difficult by opening your takeaway across the road from the local KFC and Burger King.

★ Is the location right for you as an individual? Will it be convenient for you to visit day after day or will it involve more travelling than you're willing to do on a long-term basis?

★ Is the area a reasonable one as far as demographics are concerned? Beggars can't be choosers, but going for a cheaper property can be a false economy if the insurance premium is going to be sky high and your car is going to be broken into once a week. It would also be nice to be able to get to work without feeling the need to have a can of mace always in your handbag.

★ Are there facilities available in the area which would make your working life easier? This might seem like an odd question, but having cafés, restaurants, post offices, printers and even a supermarket nearby can all help when it comes to running your own business.

★ Is there convenient parking space available in the area? If so, is this adequate or will you be likely to need more in the future?

★ Are the premises that you are considering maintained properly? It sounds ludicrous, but in our first office we had to compromise between a cheap rent and hot running water. The landlord just never got round to fixing it! We were happy to put up with it ourselves, but as we employed more people it became less than ideal.

★ Is there room to expand if you employ more staff or need to hold more stock?

★ Have you checked locally to make sure you are not being asked to pay over the odds for the property?

These are just a few of the things that you need to bear in mind when looking for premises for your business. In the 'Get the Basics' section below, you will see what your main options are when it comes to finding premises to work from.

GET THE BASICS: PREMISES – YOUR THREE MAIN OPTIONS

All businesses need somewhere to operate from and when it comes to choosing premises, you have three main options: you can work from home, you can lease or you can buy. Let's take a look at the pros and cons of each of these options.

Working from home

Working from home is becoming increasingly popular and it isn't at all difficult to understand why. To begin with, you already have your home, so there's no need to spend more money than you're currently paying on your regular mortgage. Then there's the convenience that working from home allows. For example, there's no early morning commute through rush-hour traffic because you're already on site as soon as you get out of bed. It is also easier than ever to have a 'virtual office' and use your mobile phone, web mail, a PO box or even call-handling or mail-handling agencies to be your customers' points of contact.

Of course, working from home isn't all good news and it just isn't practical for some businesses. If your business requires more space than you have in your home, or facilities that you can't easily accommodate in a domestic building, it's a non-starter. And then you have to consider clients. Even if you're willing to have them visit you at home, is this the kind of image that will make you look unprofessional? Some service businesses that specialise in helping clients remotely, such as life coaching, telesales, secretarial freelancing and copy-writing, are perfectly suited to being based in a home office. But other businesses, especially ones that involve frequent visits from clients or any kind of manufacturing process, might be better served by having separate premises to accommodate them.

If you do decide to start up your business from home, be sure to find out whether this will affect your mortgage and any existing insurance policies you may have. There are companies that specialise in providing insurance for home-workers, but you shouldn't assume that a standard 'building and contents' policy will cover anything used for business purposes. In fact, running a business from home could void certain policies altogether, so check your paperwork closely.

Finally, be aware that there may be local government restrictions on whether or not you will be permitted to run a business from home, especially if it will create any kind of disturbance to neighbours (such as noise pollution). You should therefore ask your local council for details of any restrictions that are in force.

Leasing

Just as you can rent a home instead of buying, so you can lease commercial property for the purposes of running a business. The advantages of leasing include:

★ Lower up-front costs. Whereas buying a property demands a hefty down-payment, leasing doesn't. As long as you can afford the cost of the lease itself and any associated service charges, that's all you need to get started.

★ Easier exit options. If you lease your premises and later decide that you don't want them, either because you've changed your business plans or because you simply want to get premises in another location, you won't have to worry about selling the property. Instead, you can simply give notice according to the terms and conditions of your lease agreement.

★ Right to renewal. As long as you adhere to the rules and regulations of your specific leasing agreement, you have the right to renew the lease when it expires. This means that you could effectively lease for the lifetime of your business and never have to worry about the landlord changing his or her mind.

However, there are also a few downsides to leasing that need to be considered:

★ Over the long term, leasing will prove to be more expensive than buying, simply because you never actually own any of the property you use. Your lease payments only buy you the use of the property for a specific period of time.

★ Not all leases are equal. You will need to get a solicitor to go over the details of a lease before signing on the dotted line. If you don't do this, you could make a decision you quickly regret, simply because the contract isn't fair.

Buying

The third of your three options is actually to buy a commercial property. In this case, the advantages are as follows:

★ Mortgage payments for commercial properties are often just as cheap – if not cheaper – than lease payments.

★ Every mortgage payment you make increases the amount of equity you own. When the mortgage is paid off, the property is yours. And, just like residential properties, the value of commercial properties tends to appreciate considerably over the long term. This means that your business property is making a profit in addition to the business itself.

★ You have more freedom in the way you use the property. For example, you could make structural improvements or modify the building to accommodate the specific needs of your business.

As always, there are also a few less advantageous things to take into account when choosing this option:

★ You will need to spend time and money organising the maintenance of the building. With a leased property, maintenance is generally carried out by the landlord, even if you make a financial contribution via a service charge. When you buy a commercial property, you have to organise and pay for maintenance work yourself.

★ You will need to commit a fair amount of capital to the property. If you have plenty of cash reserves to begin with, using a substantial chunk as a deposit on a commercial property might not be a problem. But if – like many business start-ups – you don't have considerable financial resources at the outset, buying a property could put you under a lot of undue pressure.

★ If you decide to sell up your business at some stage or relocate your premises, you will have to sell the property as well. This might not take long if you're in an area where commercial property is in demand, but if you aren't, or the market for your particular type of building slows down, you could be in for a long wait.

Of the three options described here, it has to be said that the first two are the most popular with those who are new to starting a business, so – unless you have bags of cash to start with – those are the ones we'd be most likely to recommend.

WORKING FROM HOME – OUR OWN EXPERIENCE

REBECCA SAYS:

When Kirsty and I started out with Gapwork, we began by working from my house. The main reason we did this was because it was the most economical option and, at the time, we didn't actually need any more space. I also had a toddler to deal with, who would either be looked after by a childminder at home, or at a nursery for a couple of mornings a week. It was a nice way of easing myself into the frame of mind of a working mum, without my daughter being put into full-time childcare.

Working from home can be tricky though, particularly as you tend to get easily distracted (or at least I did) by making lunch, coffee and taking care of all the domestic chores which are sitting there awaiting attention while you are trying to work. Also, in the summer it is tempting to hold spontaneous meetings in the garden or knock off work early to get the barbecue sorted.

More seriously, working from home meant that there were no clearly defined working hours. This was made worse by the fact that I was doing a lot of work late at night when my daughter had gone to bed. This isn't really a healthy way of getting things done, and I did find it stressful. You are constantly wearing two hats – one is the mum at home and the other is the professional person in the workplace. While this is bearable in the short term, it means that you aren't as effective as you could be in either role, because each one really needs its own separate commitment of focused time and attention.

In the end, it was a relief when we found our first offices nearby. In an ideal world, our work would be so closely linked to our personal wellbeing and development that there wouldn't need to be a defining line between work and home life. But in the real world as it stands, you need to be able to take off your 'professional' hat when you walk through your front door and put on your 'at home' hat. This approach just makes it a lot easier to deal with the very different pressures that our work and home lives put on us as individuals.

From a purely practical point of view, having to split the telephone and Internet bills between things that my family was paying for and things that the company was paying for was also a hassle. It made us look less professional having a hotmail e-mail address, having a domestic address on our business stationery and not being sure if the phone was ringing because my Mum wanted to remind me of my Dad's birthday, or because an important client wanted to discuss the latest project. So it became obvious fairly quickly that we needed to find an office. Buying was not an option for financial reasons, so we started to look for a office we could rent.'

OFFICE HUNTING

We soon realised that, being a start-up, finding office space was not as easy as we thought it would be. The main stumbling blocks for us were the cost of the rent and the length of the lease. Our first office was actually quite easy from a convenience point of view because it was rented to us on a 'tenancy at will' agreement, which basically meant that we only had to give the landlord a week's notice if we decided to move on. Of course, the same also applied in reverse, so the landlord could have given us just a week's notice if he'd wanted to get rid of us. However, the rent was cheap and there were plenty of other rooms that we could expand into if the need arose. As it turned out, this was just as well: when we moved in we employed one person, then within two years we had employed another 12 members of staff!

But, as we mentioned earlier, you do generally get what you pay for. The offices were in a 1960s block above a take-away, a fish shop and a freezer shop that sold everything for under a pound. There were about four flights of stairs to our offices and no lift, so when we had a delivery of magazines or books we would have to create a human chain to get all the products up the stairs. The toilets were so cold in winter that you tried to avoid sitting on the seat whenever possible, and giving directions to visitors was always hilarious: 'Just go past the bookies on the left and you'll see a Netto's store next to some charity shops. We are opposite the Co-op supermarket above the fish shop.' Not exactly the kind of corporate glam-our we would have liked!

After we had bought out the investors, we knew that we wanted to work in an environment that wasn't freezing in winter and boiling in summer and that didn't scare visitors when they arrived after dark on winter evenings. We contacted a huge number of estate agents and were quickly (and unfairly) dismissed as serious tenants because of the fact we were a start-up. The estate agents would show up in their shiny BMWs and we would be there waiting next to Kirsty's Fiesta, which she had bought from her Mum. They'd look us up and down and make an instant judgement – probably not related to the fact we were female, in retrospect, but because we had 'start-up' written all over us. We were under the age of 30 at the time and didn't have any of the trappings of successful business women (at least in the eyes of estate agents). Because of this we would often find ourselves hounding estate agents after a viewing, practically throwing money at them. More often than not, they didn't return our calls or persuade us to make an appointment for a second viewing.

Then one day, we were getting a lunchtime sandwich in the part of Leeds where we wanted to find an office. Purely by chance we spotted a board outside a house saying 'offices to rent'. So we climbed over the wall to find out more, not realising that there was a road at the back of the house which the main entrance faced. The shortest lease we could negotiate was for three years with a two-year break clause. This meant that after two years we could opt out. We had been going for a few years by this time and knew that the company had at least another two years in it, so we signed up. After months of searching for a new office, we had found one by chance and were able to move in within six weeks.

Why bother renting premises?

When you are first setting up your own business, you need to be realistic about the amount of time you will actually be spending at work. Even if you are lucky and end up working 40 hours a week or less, it will still be a significant amount of time that you spend at work over the course of a few months or a year. For this reason it is important to choose a workplace which isn't too lonely or miles from anywhere – one that is safe, warm and dry and that you can make your own.

Most of us have worked in a bland, boring, noisy, smelly environment at some point in our lives. The brilliant thing about setting up your own business is that you don't have to stick with the status quo. You can raise the bar and make your workplace one that you will actually look forward to spending time in. A haven, or a refuge even.

Think about all the things that you might have hated about workspaces before you had a choice in the matter. The fact that you had no privacy. No office of your own. Maybe not even a desk of your own. Or it could be that you were *too* alone and could have benefited from working more closely with your colleagues. The décor might have been drab and grey and so blandly uniform that the whole place felt more like a prison than somewhere to work. Maybe the lights flickered and were never fixed properly, giving you a throbbing headache that lasted all day. Or maybe the smell of rancid coffee, stale crisps and Bombay Bad Boy Pot Noodles wafted into your environment from the next room. Oh yes, we've been there and experienced all of that.

When you are choosing a workplace from scratch for your own business, you have the freedom to change all this. You don't need to be able to afford a polished marble floor, a fountain in the foyer or a couple of handsome doormen to greet your visitors. Even with a fairly limited budget you can do quite a lot to make your workplace the kind of environment you look forward to visiting each day.

Look around to find somewhere that maybe has a great view out of the windows. Buy some of your favourite flowers or plants. Paint the whole place with your favourite colour (although you may want to check this with your landlord first). Hang some beautiful pictures on the walls or some inspiring quotes from people you admire. Get a desk of your own. And maybe a desk toy, if that appeals to you. How about a Newton's Cradle? Or a desktop Zen garden? Whatever your personal tastes and preferences, fill your workspace with positive things so it is somewhere that you want to spend time.

You should aim to create an environment that is so comfortable and appealing that you actually look forward to going to work in the morning, otherwise what is the point of working for yourself? If you want to be miserable at work there are thousands of employers who can make it happen for you in a heartbeat!

It is important that your workplace reflects you as an individual in some way and your business as an extension of that. We're not recommending that you make your office look like your front room, and clearly the space needs to convey the fact that you are a professional person with a dynamic business, but this is your chance to create your own working environment. It would be a massive shame to waste it.

DEIRDRE BOUNDS, FOUNDER OF I-TO-I

If you have a small budget, go to Regional Development Agencies (RDAs) or Business Link to find out if there is any business incubator space available. Always look for a short-term lease and try not to get involved with a long-term lease. I would never take on anything that had a break clause at five years or after. Work on a three-year plan and ensure that the spaces you are looking at are big enough for expansion, or are in a building where expansion is a possibility. On the other hand, don't take out a lease on a building which is too large.

When you are pricing up the lease, remember to factor in landlord's repairs and service charges, as well as rates and solicitors' fees. Never pay landlord's solicitors fees for arranging the lease. This can add 30 per cent onto your first year's rent. This practice is rarely operated these days, although landlords will always try.

In most cities, there seems to be plenty of office space on the market. Use your negotiating skills to pitch for anything from a rent-free period to getting more PC points put in or having the décor updated. I would always use a good firm of solicitors to secure the lease for me. In my experience, city centre offices aren't all they are cracked up to be. Parking and rents are always extortionate there, and as long as the place is easy to find, looks presentable and has parking, most visitors would prefer not to have to come to the city centre.

Visit i-to-i online at: www.i-to-i.com

Due diligence

Some businesses, by their very nature, will need particular types of premises. Anything involving factories, shops or nurseries will need to have appropriate buildings. In these cases it is particularly important that you check all aspects of the property before signing a lease. This is what solicitors call 'due diligence' and it means that you check the following elements of a lease at the very least:

★ That the person who is offering you the lease is actually entitled to do so.

★ That the terms and conditions of the lease are all clearly defined and clarified in the official lease document.

★ Make sure that you are clear about how much money you are paying, who you will be paying, when you will be paying and when future rent reviews will take place.

★ Check how long the lease is for and how much notice you need to give to vacate the property, as well as how much notice the landlord has to give you to leave. Be clear on what form any such notice is to be given in and try to make sure that written notice is specified.

★ Check and understand who will be liable to pay for damages, repairs and insurance on the property. Also check who will be responsible for actually carrying out any necessary repairs.

★ Likewise, check and understand who will be liable for business rates, utility bills and service charges.

★ Make sure that the property is suitable for the kind of business you want to operate within it and that you have all the planning permissions that may be required to run such a business from there.

★ Check to see what happens when the lease runs out. Will you be able to get another one automatically or not? Also, how long is the landlord's leasehold of the property?

★ Will you be able to sublet any of the property?

★ Find out who will be liable to pay the legal costs of the landlord. If it is you, how much will they be and can you negotiate them down to a lower amount?

★ Is there any kind of personal guarantee involved in taking on the lease? For example, will you be putting your home at risk if you are unable to adhere to the lease agreement? We ourselves would avoid any lease which involves personal liability, but they do exist, so check before you sign.

★ What happens if you want to get out of the lease at any point? Is there a break clause or can you sub-let it to someone else?

It is always useful to have some legal advice when signing a lease – especially when it involves any kind of personal guarantee. Business and commercial leases are often much more complex and varied than those for residential property, so having an experienced eye on your side can be very helpful. Shop around for a good solicitor. Get some initial free advice from them, see if you like them, then get them to quote you on how much they will charge to advise you on the lease. Try to get at least three different quotes from different solicitors. The Law Society has a useful website and service called Lawyers For Your Business. As well as featuring helpful downloadable fact sheets, you can access a free half-hour consultation with a solicitor. Find out more at **www.lfyb.lawsociety.org.uk**.

Tip: With leases, most things are negotiable – particularly if the market is on a downturn and the landlord is keen to rent the property quickly. Don't sign anything until you know exactly what your commitment is and you are happy with the terms and conditions. Also, bear in mind that you will probably be asked for references by the landlord. These could come from previous landlords, banks, accountants, solicitors or suppliers with whom you have had longstanding trading relationships.

HOW TO FIND BUSINESS PREMISES

We found our offices on both occasions by snooping around the areas where we wanted to find space. To do this effectively, you need to keep a pen and paper handy at all times (for scribbling down phone numbers of estate agents) and a mobile phone for ringing them there and then. It's best to do this at times when the traffic isn't too heavy as it invariably involves slamming your brakes on, swerving into the kerb and parking illegally while you write down the contact details from an estate agent's sign outside the premises. Trying to find the right space on the right terms can be difficult and time consuming, so try not to let it interfere too much with other things going on in your business. Other ways of finding office space include:

★ Word of mouth – tell everyone you meet what you are looking for and ask if they know of anything suitable. You'd be surprised how effective this can be, especially if you are talking to other businesses.

★ Read the commercial property ads in local newspapers.

★ Phone local estate agents and leave your details and an outline of what you are looking for with each of them. (Don't hold your breath for them to get back to you though. Unless the market is slow they won't be very proactive.)

★ Contact your local council and find out if they rent out business premises. Some councils own low-rent commercial properties which they reserve for start-ups, although there is often a waiting list for such property.

★ Business Link and other regional or local business support agencies often have information about commercial premises on their books.

★ Sub-let space from another company. This can work well as long as you get on with the main leaseholders and they are allowed to sub-let under the terms of their lease. Such a lease should be really flexible so that if it doesn't work out, or if either you or the main leaseholder expand and want to move on, you can do so.

Serviced offices

If you require more than a mobile number, a home address and a PC to run your business, but you can't go the whole hog and take out a long-term lease, it may be worth considering serviced offices as an option. There are many of these across the country and they provide space, Internet connections, meeting places, parking and professional facilities to all kinds of businesses. The leases are often shorter term (between three and 12 months) and not as onerous as those for normal commercial property.

Serviced offices offer increased flexibility to small businesses whose needs may change rapidly. The amount of space you want or need to take is flexible, as are the services you choose to take up. It may be that you need a 'stop-gap' between working from home and taking on a longer-term lease, and in this case serviced offices could be an option. The rent in these kind of offices may be more expensive than the rent on a longer-term lease, but then you don't have to worry about decorating before you move in, adding phone lines, Internet connections or arranging maintenance and upkeep of the property. To find out more about serviced offices in your area, simply look in the Yellow Pages or go to **www.yell.com**.

TO SUM UP . . .

★ Take time to consider carefully what you are looking for from your new premises.

★ If you want to work from home, think through all the implications.

★ Never take a lease at face value. Read the small print.

★ Think ahead – you may need to expand in the near future, but at the same time don't take on somewhere that is too big.

★ Make your office into an environment where you want to spend time.

★ Look at all the ways you can research potential premises – estate agents aren't always the best option.

5

Growing Your Business: Marketing

WHEN YOU CREATED YOUR BUSINESS PLAN, you should have done so with future growth in mind. Nobody starts a business with the intention of having it tread water or pootle along at a snail's pace (well, nobody who seriously expects to succeed at any rate), so strong and sustainable growth should always be the aim of the entrepreneurial start-up.

To achieve this growth in the real world, you will need a number of things:

★ Skills and resources, usually obtained from the manpower you hire. We covered this in some detail in Chapter 3, so there is no need to repeat ourselves here.

★ An increase in the number of sales you make. Different organisations will naturally define sales in different ways, but at the heart of every business there is a transaction between it and the customer, which brings in the revenue. This is the one crucial relationship you need to build.

In order to grow your business you will need to develop your relationships with existing customers, so they come back to you and recommend you to others. You will also need to find new customers from scratch. The aim of this chapter is to discuss effective ways of pursuing both of these goals.

IDENTIFY YOUR MARKET

Before you can even begin to consider the specifics of marketing your business, you first need to spend time thinking carefully about who you want to market to. In other words, who are your customers and where are you most likely to find them? You should already have a fairly clear picture of your target customer from writing your business plan, but it is vital that before you come up with any marketing or communications strategy you go back to that plan and remind yourself about exactly who your customers are. The vaguer you are on this topic, the harder it will be to market in a truly effective way.

For example, if you are selling a baby product online, it is the easiest thing in the world to say 'the potential market for my products is the x million people who either have a baby, or who are thinking of having a baby'. However, it would be the hardest thing in the world actually to target such a vague market and tell these 'x million' people about your product.

A better approach by far is to start with a niche. The way we started out with Gapwork is a very good example of this. We began by creating a website which would be targeted at everyone aged 16–30 who was interested in travelling to Australia and Europe, or who was already out there. We had some initial success in communicating with this market by posting messages about the service on traveller chat forums and creating useful e-mails which people could forward to each other.

But it soon became apparent that without a massive marketing budget (bearing in mind our initial investment was just £15,000 and this also had to cover wages and other costs), we would not be able to reach even a fraction of our market effectively – certainly not enough people to make our business as successful as we wanted it to be. The challenge then was to look at our product and look at the market, and come up with a more effective channel through which we could sell our product.

The website subscription model wasn't going to be able to reach the required number of people in order to make money. So we looked at all the content on the site and thought, 'What if it was an offline product? A book?'

This opened up a whole new vista. We followed up by thinking, 'Who would buy a book about gap years for young people?' Obviously the young people themselves would, but we would still have to find the handful of those who were actually considering travelling to make the sale from a huge market. So, who else would buy the book? The obvious answer was schools. They have young people in them, as well as easily identifiable purchasers of the product – librarians and careers officers, for example.

Based on this fresh insight, we created our own database of secondary schools in the United Kingdom (using all public domain information) and sent out a mailer to heads of careers promoting our gap year book. Magically, the faxed order forms started to come back to us. We had hit upon a niche market where there was clear demand for our products. This, then, was the foundation of our business at Gapwork.

As you can see, identifying your market as 'every person between the ages of 16 and 30 who wants to travel and work in Australia and Europe' is not much use. Unless you are

Virgin or Apple, you are not going to be able to promote your products or services to this many people. But identifying your market as 'careers teachers and librarians in UK secondary schools' is an altogether more manageable proposition.

FIND A CHANNEL TO YOUR MARKET

'Channel' sounds a bit like marketing blurb, but actually it describes perfectly the medium required for promoting your products or services to potential customers or clients. Basically, what we are talking about here are ways to tell your customer how brilliant your business is. A channel can also mean the way in which a customer is able to buy your products, and the two meanings do overlap occasionally. For example, a website is a way to tell people about your business, but it can also enable customers buy your products.

One business can have lots of different channels to market. At Gapwork, we use a combination of mailers, telemarketing and events to give us different ways into the schools market. Other publishers use catalogues or sales reps. On our websites, we use a combination of links from other sites, Google Adwords, search engine optimisation and affiliate links. If these terms are unfamiliar don't worry, we will talk about them in more detail shortly. There are many ways of using channels to market and, inevitably, some will not work for you.

LOUISE GOULDING, FOUNDER OF SHAREMYMEMORY.COM

Sharemymemory.com provides personalised websites for life's special moments. Our three main services are baby, wedding and memorial websites, and we also offer gift certificates. This makes marketing quite a challenge: the market is potentially very big, but there are at least three sectors to target and our competitors include big brands such as Microsoft.

Within weeks of the website going live at **www. sharemymemory.com**, we began a closely targeted campaign involving PR, events, search engine optimisation, web and print advertising, direct mail and more. This was measured through promotional codes printed on brochures and adverts and monitoring website traffic.

Two activities stand out as having provided an excellent return on investment – PR opportunities and partnerships. Exhibiting at Yorkshire Brides in Harrogate helped us get involved in the ITV Calendar Wedding, where we provided a personalised wedding website for the winning couple. We sent out press releases before the event and organised a stunt on the day involving people dressed as bride and groom teddy bears. Search engine optimisation ensured that anyone looking for the Calendar Wedding found Sharemymemory.com, and we used the exhibitors' mailing list for a follow-up direct mail campaign with a range of special offers.

Partnerships have also helped us to target niche markets. Our partnership with Charities Trust means that their 8,000 member charities can help their clients set up memorial websites, complete with online donations, and benefit from 15 per cent revenue share from Sharemymemory.com. For **Expatsreunite.com**, a website with over 60,000 visitors a month, we offer its members a way to keep in touch with friends and family abroad and a 15 per cent discount at Sharemymemory.com. With Pink Products, we have launched a new website targeted specifically at the gay market.

The major advantage of our service is that it is viral – anyone creating a website for a special person or event with

Sharemymemory.com will send their friends and family to it. This means that word of mouth will become an increasingly powerful marketing tool for us as we grow.

Visit sharemymemory.com at:
www.sharemymemory.com

With planning, you can reduce the risk of starting with a channel to market that won't work for you.

Once you have identified your target market, you need to start thinking about the best ways to reach that market. The hardest thing to do is to communicate with an undefined audience. As a start-up you are unlikely to have access to multi-million-pound marketing budgets that would allow you to advertise on TV, radio and billboards in city centres. So, if you have a product that is relevant for hospital trust managers, you need to look at what conferences or events they attend and what publications they read. The most common marketing channels, in a general sense, are:

★ print media – magazines, newspapers, journals, newsletters, direct mail
★ digital media – online, e-mails, forums, mobile phones, CD-ROM and DVD
★ broadcast media – TV and radio
★ wholesalers, agents, brokers and resellers

One way of working out what channel to market will work for your business is to draw a large spider diagram (also referred to as a 'mind map'; this concept was created by Tony Buzan) with your business at the centre of it. Then, with your customers in mind, draw offshoots from the centre which represent different ways in which the customers might get to hear about your business.

So for example:

Hodgson Dog Accessories

Customers: UK dog owners with a certain amount of disposable income to pamper their pooches with.

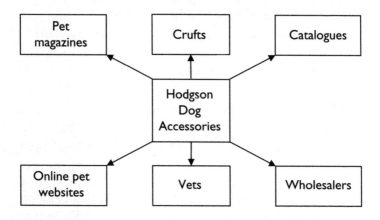

Don't be afraid to brainstorm and put things on the diagram that aren't immediately obvious. At a later stage you'll be able to think about what is practical.

Some businesses will only have one main channel to market. A dairy farmer may only sell products to the supermarkets, for example. This means he or she has less to worry about in terms of planning a marketing strategy, but it can be high risk; if the supermarkets suddenly find a cheaper supplier, they could decide to switch.

Always try to learn from other successful businesses in a similar field to yours. What are they doing that is working effectively for them? What are they doing that you think could be improved upon? There is nothing wrong with learning from other people's successes and mistakes.

Many businesses (and especially small start-ups) will need to have a number of channels to market. The decision in this case is prioritising which will be the most effective channel to focus on. Once you have brainstormed every possible option for getting your products or services sold, you then need to draw up a list with some pros and cons. For example, Hodgson Dog Accessories' list might look something like this:

Channel	Pros	Cons
Pet magazines	large readership	expensive
Crufts	targeted audience	competition
Catalogues	cheap to implement	low product profile
Online pet websites	cheap and popular	difficult to convert to sales
Vets	understand product	logistically hard work
Wholesalers	easy to set up	low profit margin

You will soon see what is practical from a marketing point of view. Some things will be too expensive. Others will be too risky. Most will take a lot of time to implement. Let's take a look at each of the channels mentioned earlier in this chapter and see what the implications of each one are.

Print media
Newspapers
Newspapers are useful for advertising certain sorts of products and services. You will have seen advertisements for jobs, writing courses, holidays and household products included in relevant sections. Whether your particular products or services would get a response by being advertised in a newspaper

totally depends on its readership profile. You can find out more about the number and type of people that read that newspaper by asking the advertising department for a media pack. Simply ring them up, explain that you want to advertise and ask them to send you a media pack. This should provide you with more information about the typical reader, and you'll be able to tell whether they would be interested in your product or service.

Another good idea is to visit the online National Readership Survey at **www.nrs.co.uk**. Here you will see that reader profiles are broken down by gender, age and ABC1 socio-demographic gradings. The latter is a way of classifying people according to their occupation and perceived social class. This might seem a bit stereotypical, but it is useful from a marketing and media planning point of view.

For example, if you are running a business selling cheap stag weekend holidays in Benidorm or Magaluf, you would probably find advertising in the *Sun* to be fairly effective, as it has a large readership made up of mostly men aged 15–44 in the C2DE social grading. (In case you're wondering, C2DE social grades include manual workers, supervisory, clerical, junior management and casual workers.) The drawback to advertising in a newspaper with a circulation like the *Sun* is that you would be paying a lot for advertising. But if you had the necessary budget, it could be money well spent.

Magazines

Whereas newspapers have fairly broad readerships, magazines are more focused. People buy newspapers to read today's news. They buy magazines to read about fashion, music, cars, fishing or whatever else their particular interest is. There is obviously no reason for advertising a baby product in a fishing magazine. But the NRS website can help you make decisions about magazines and their readerships too. Again, you should also ask for media packs. Circulations differ widely within women's magazines, but unless you are looking at the box ads in the back of glossy magazines, placing an advert elsewhere in these kind of publications can be prohibitively expensive.

If you are working in a particular field that has well known newsletters or journals that are sent out to your target market, it may be worth contacting them to get an idea about the advertising opportunities that are available. They won't have the big circulations of glossy national magazines, but the specific nature of the audience subscribing to the periodical will often lead to better results for your advert.

Remember that everything is negotiable and it is always worth haggling with media sales people – if only to help make their jobs more interesting. Don't just try to negotiate for a lower price, but go for the best possible positioning for your advert too. Generally speaking, adverts on the right hand page stand out more than those on the left. While you're at it, try to haggle the salesperson into increasing the size of your ad space wherever possible, and getting colour advertising (for the same price as black and white) where you can.

Direct mail

Direct mail is an extremely useful way of communicating with your customers. The British postal service comes in very handy when it comes to mailing information to punters. Unfortunately, direct mail is also very easy to get wrong and we have learned a lot through trial and error in our postal communications with schools in the past.

Schools and teachers are tricky because they get so much mail. Head teachers and heads of department in particular will either bin something immediately if they think it is junk mail, or put it on their pile of 'stuff to read later', which inevitably never gets read. And that is if they receive it at all. Sometimes the school secretary will automatically bin a mailer, thinking of it as junk mail, as soon as it arrives.

It is a good discipline to assume that all of your customers (in whatever business you run) are equally overloaded with information coming through the post. Operating from this perspective means that you have to make your direct mailshots really stand out from the crowd and make the recipient want to open it immediately.

The trick here is to make your direct mailshot really relevant. Try to get the timing right. For example, if you are a tax advisor and you want to get business from people having to complete their self-assessment forms, send out your mailer a couple of months before the deadline and put a big headline on it saying something like 'Need help with your self assessment? The deadline is looming!'. As long as your customers have to fill in a self-assessment form, and as long as they haven't already done it, your letter will be relevant to them. It is the relevance of your communication which is the most important thing – make sure the mail is going out to the right person at the right time.

The look and feel of the direct mailshot is also important, although this is more true for some markets than for others. For our own market, for example, it is still not as important as getting the right message to the right person at the right time. We have sent out full-colour glossy catalogues and had less response than when we have sent photocopied, single-sided black and white letters. The reason for this in schools may be that full-colour catalogues are ten a penny and teachers can't be bothered to read them all.

There are some basic things that are important to get right in direct mail, whatever your business.

★ Give your message a beginning, a middle and an end. Start with an eye-catching strapline raising the issue. Follow this with information about how your product or service can resolve this issue for the reader, and end with a 'call to action' – 'Contact Fred on 0800 XXX for more information', or something along those lines.

★ Regardless of how colourful, glossy and slick the visual presentation of your mailing is, if there are any spelling or grammatical mistakes – even one – it is more likely to be binned. Because of this, it makes sense to get someone to proofread the mailshot for you before you send it out. Even better, get five people to proofread it for you.

★ Don't forget to put your contact details on the mailing. You'd be surprised how easy it is to forget the most important things when you are rushing around running your own business, but if the client doesn't know how to contact you, they won't be able to buy, no matter how much they want to.

★ Get the recipient's name and contact details right. There is nothing that peeves people more than receiving mailings with incorrect personal information. After all, if you can't even get the recipient's name right, why should they believe that you can do anything else right? In direct mail, as in life itself, first impressions are extremely important. So make a good one!

★ Start the text of the mailing with a statement or a question that is direct and to the point. The recipient will thank you for not making them waste their time reading something that turns out not to be relevant to them. Of course, if you've targeted your recipients properly, sending out irrelevant mailshots shouldn't be something that happens regularly.

★ Put positive stuff in your mailings – great reviews of your product or service, positive feedback and recommendations go a long way to help the reader develop confidence in your business. You should also include details of any awards, professional seals of approval or memberships of professional bodies. When you are a start-up you need all the help you can get to get yourself taken seriously.

★ Talk about the customer as much as about yourself. Don't focus on blowing your own trumpet, but on telling the recipient how you can help them. Always remember that all of your potential customers have 'WIIFM' stamped on their foreheads – which stands for 'What's In It For Me?' Answer that question in your mailshot and you'll be half way there.

★ Make it really easy for the reader to understand the purpose of the mailing. Don't confuse them by mixing too many messages. Brevity and clarity should be your watchwords at all times.

GET THE BASICS: WRITING MARKETING COPY

The written word is one of the most powerful tools a business has when it comes to marketing. Whether it's an advertisement for a local newspaper, a sales letter for a direct mail campaign, a page for a website or a promotional e-mail, how you write your copy will have a big impact on its success.

Professional copywriters adopt two main principles when writing marketing copy. First, they aim to make sure that the copy is customer-oriented. In other words, don't waste time (and marketing money) telling the reader how great or fascinating your business is, or giving your life story. Instead, focus on telling readers how your product or service will be able to benefit *them*.

The second thing professionals do is to follow a specific copywriting structure, generally represented by the acronym 'AIDA'. This stands for Attention, Interest, Desire and Action. Let us take you through each step of this structure so you can use it whenever you need to write effective marketing copy.

Attention

The first thing you need to do in any piece of marketing copy, whether it's intended for print or online distribution, is to grab the attention of the reader. If it's appropriate, use a strong, eye-catching headline that makes the reader take a personal interest in the copy, then follow up with an equally strong opening paragraph. It's essential here that you make the opening as customer oriented as you can. So, instead of writing a headline 'Why Our Organically Grown Apples Are the Healthiest in the World', you would do much better to write 'How Eating Organically Grown Apples Can Help You Live Longer'. The first headline is very 'company' oriented, but in the second the focus is clearly on the benefits to the customer and it is therefore much more likely to get his or her attention.

Interest

Having got the attention of your reader, the next thing you need to do is develop their interest further. You do this by maintaining your focus on the customer while at the same time revealing more information about your product or service. For example, instead of simply giving a dull account of scientific research that links organically grown fruit with good health, you could phrase the copy so that it reads as a list of direct benefits to the reader. So you put, 'Researchers in Germany have proven that eating five servings of organically grown fruit each day can boost your immune system by up to 25 per cent!' Obviously this is a fictional claim for the purposes of illustration, but it does show how writing with the reader in mind makes the copy more appealing and develops interest.

Desire

Once interest has been established, your third task is to make the reader desire the product or service that you have to offer. One of the best ways to do this is by using a case study which shows how someone else has benefited. For example, if you have a client who experienced a range of health benefits after switching to your brand of organically grown apples, you could use this person's experience to show how your product helped to improve his or her life.

This approach to building desire works because human beings are always envious of other people who succeed in some way. By saying 'Mary achieved this using our product' or 'Natalie hired our services and gained that', the reader almost automatically begins to say, 'I want to do that too!'

Action

When you have built up a strong sense of desire in your reader, it's time to invite him or her to take action. This is where you 'close the sale' by asking them to request more details about your service, place an order for your product or otherwise make the kind of response you want them to make. When you do this, be sure to encourage an immediate response, as if they don't take action right there and then, the chances of them doing so some time later are extremely small. Offering time-limited special deals or free bonuses if they order immediately or within a certain number of days will compel the reader to get off the fence and decide whether or not he or she wants to respond.

Online media

There are two very different sides to any discussion of business and online media. On one side, you can discuss having an online presence (namely, a website) that helps your offline business. And on the other side, you can discuss having an actual online business. If your business is entirely online, then only bits of what we are about to say in this section will be relevant for you. But it's probably worth reading anyway, simply because when we started, our website was our business and it was only because it wasn't working that we developed the business to run offline.

We certainly don't claim to be online marketing gurus, but we can share what we know has worked for us, along with the things that haven't. When we started Gapwork.com, we paid a web designer £500 to put a few pages together that would convey information to the reader in an easy way and also provide space for advertising. It is always worth finding a designer, whose work you like, to come up with some visual ideas. Even if you know exactly how you want your website to work and you are a whiz at the technical side, a good web designer will produce a look and feel which makes your site look professional and appealing. As with print designers, write down exactly what you want (your 'brief'), and let them come back to you with ideas and costs. Always get at least three quotes from three different designers so that you get a fair idea of the costs involved. If you can't afford a professional web designer, try students at colleges or start-ups who may be willing to do the work for less money as they are building their portfolios. We have never looked through the Yellow Pages and selected the first design agency whose advert we like the look of, and neither should you. Instead, spend some time shopping around a bit and you may find someone who is talented, creative, on your wavelength and who is more cost effective than a swanky agency that inevitably has much higher overheads.

So, let's begin with a question: what do you want your website to do for you? If it is a 'channel' to your market (in the sense that you want people to be able to find you online and discover more about what you do), then you need the website to look good, work well and – most importantly – be easy to use. This means going out of your way to avoid the common mistakes that businesses often make when creating a website to market themselves. The main mistakes we are referring to are:

★ Letting the techies run the show and ending up with a super-slick, Flash-based site that the user doesn't feel in control of. There is nothing worse than trying to find a company's contact details on a website which starts with a two-minute intro and then blinds you with design wizardry. Just give users your phone number, or at least have a 'skip intro' button that they can use to bypass the fireworks show.

★ Having a 'contact us' page which consists of just an e-mail form. E-mail forms mean that the visitor has no alternative but to fill them in and then wait for a reply – but most customers expect instant responses and information.

★ Having a website which is difficult to read or plays hell with the eyes. We are obsessive about keeping things super clear and easy. Dark text on a light background, please, if it is something you want us to read. Likewise the font needs to be large enough to read. And watch the colour schemes. We're sure we aren't alone in believing that red and green stripes give people headaches.

★ Utilising a website navigation system that is at all complicated or difficult to understand. While this might win the techie an award for 'Pointless but Impressive Over-Use of Code', it isn't good for business. You should always approach your customers as if they are completely unaware of how websites work. Sometimes it is hard to get designers to create sites in this way, as they tend to think that everyone is as web-savvy as they are. You have to be firm and demand that your website is designed so simply that your 90-year-old granny could use it and find her way around it without difficulty.

★ Having pop-up advertisements which obstruct the text

of your own pages. Even if the pop-ups are easy to click away, this can still put people off having a proper look at your website.

★ Publishing a website which contains spelling or grammatical mistakes. Pay someone to proofread your online text if you have to. Whatever you do, don't expect the programmers or web designers to feel responsible for getting the words right. They are techies and creatives – not usually the kind of people who can be bothered to be particularly careful when it comes to punctuation or spelling. Besides, they shouldn't really be writing any original text in the first place. That's your job – or the job of any writer you might choose to hire.

Try to begin the process of creating your businesses website with a simple goal in mind. This might be 'to sell more products', or 'to make it easy for people to find out about me', or even just 'to make my contact details available to everyone with an Internet connection and a computer'. The simpler your goal, the more likely it is that your site will be able achieve it.

We learnt an interesting lesson about websites and online business in the early days of Gapwork. When we started out, we would market ourselves by finding relevant online chat groups, message boards, forums and communities, and name drop our site. Sometimes we would be honest about our vested interest, or – when that wasn't allowed – we would disguise ourselves virtually as backpackers or gap year travellers who would then recommend our site. This was done wherever possible on a daily basis and the hits to the website gradually increased, as did requests for our e-mail newsletter and purchases of our books. What we lacked was the reach into the larger market which we knew was out there. So we paid to have the site developed and feature better e-commerce facilities and content.

When we had the all-singing, all-dancing version of the site online, we did see a slight increase in the number of visitors, but nothing major. We tried various methods for getting the site to move up the listings of Yahoo and Google, including paying a search engine optimisation company to 'tag' the pages of the website and submit it to the search engines. Then we tried changing the content to include as many keywords as possible in the content (keywords meaning those words or phrases that customers would be likely to use when searching for information online). We also set up reciprocal weblinks with loads of different companies and tried pretty much every trick in the book for getting the site up on the search engines. The results weren't instant by any means, but slowly, over time, our website did get higher up the search engines under certain keyword searches. We were also getting more hits than we had ever had before. So, it was a roaring success all round, wasn't it?

Well no, not really. Although we had more visitors than ever before and we were listed on the first page of both Google and Yahoo whenever someone carried out a search on 'work in Australia' or 'gap year', the site wasn't making any more money. In fact it was costing us more than ever, as we were paying the search engine optimisers, we were paying more for a better hosting service, we were paying for some 'pay per click'-type adverts on Google, we were spending more time updating the site as it was now so much bigger, the e-commerce section cost money, and of course there were the initial costs of designing and programming the new improved version. And we were actually selling fewer books than we did when it was a much simpler site with fewer people hitting it! This didn't seem to make sense.

We gradually realised the reasons why this was happening. Firstly, when we had been mentioning the site on message boards and chatrooms, we were marketing directly to people who were probably interested in what our website did. All right, we hadn't been reaching very many people, but those we did were exactly the sort who would then go to the website and realise that our books could save them time and money and be well worth buying. What was happening now was that every month, thousands of people were clicking through to the site after searching on Google for 'gap year', for example. But those thousands of people didn't necessarily want to go to Australia or one of the other destinations we wrote about. It was possible they were at a very early stage of planning their gap year and therefore not interested in making a financial commitment to the idea by purchasing a book. It was possible they didn't understand even what a gap year is – and the information on our site was designed for people who had decided what they wanted to do and where they wanted to go. So you can see how reaching a wider audience does not automatically mean that sales will increase.

Secondly, we had increased the amount of content on the website to the point that users might have believed they didn't need to buy the books. Why buy a book when you can read about it online for free? Obviously, we knew that the books contained lots more content than the website, but how was the customer to realise the added value of the books without actually seeing them?

Thirdly, we had made the mistake of confusing our users.

The website wasn't clear about whether it was a marketing site for our books, an information site about gap years, or just a database of advertisers. Fortunately we realised this fairly quickly and shifted the emphasis of the Gapwork site to what it is today, which is basically an information site with lots of companies on it that can help you have a great gap year. The beauty of this model is that as long as we maintain the number of visitors to the site and keep it easy to use, our advertisers will always get interested people clicking through to their sites. We still sell our books online, but really this is now more a sideline than a priority.

So the message here is simple – getting thousands of people hitting your website isn't automatically going to equate to thousands of sales, unless the site has been created with a simple goal in mind and is kept focused on that goal. And even then you won't necessarily get those sales. When you think of how many people use the Internet and how random it can be, you will see that it is a very tricky channel to get right. Without a simple goal, a decent designer who understands that goal and a development plan that is cast in stone, websites can become extremely distracting, expensive and time-consuming.

GET THE BASICS: SEARCH ENGINE OPTIMISATION

Optimising your website so that it is ranked higher by the popular search engines such as Google and Yahoo doesn't have to be an overly complicated business. In fact, there are several simple things you can do to optimise your website in a day or two . . .

★ Try to include at least one key word in your domain name. For example, if you sell chocolate teddy bears, having **www.chocolateteddy.co.uk** as your domain name would be more effective than www.ctb.co.uk, as the former would be identified by a search engine whenever anyone looked for 'chocolate teddy'.

★ Include key words on your home page. Don't use the old-fashioned idea of having a block of 'invisible' key words at the bottom of your home page. Instead, work key words into your introductory text. For example, the first line on your home page could be 'Welcome to the world of chocolate teddy bears!' And so on.

★ Include reciprocal links. Offer an associated (but non-competitive) organisation a link to their website in return for them providing a link back to you. The more websites you have with a link to your own site, the higher you will rank in search engine results pages, as the engine views your site as being more popular.

★ Use the ALT tag to associate key words with any images on your site. Search engine spiders can't read images, but they can read text – so as well as showing a picture of a chocolate teddy, attach the key words 'chocolate teddy' to that picture.

★ Write articles about your business and deposit them in online article repositories such as www.articlecity.com. If you ensure that you include a link to your website at the end of any article you write, you get all the benefits of a reciprocal link without having to find anyone to reciprocate with!

There are other search engine optimisation techniques you could employ, but these five steps will get you off to the best possible start with a minimum of time or expense. Bear in mind that the major search engines (which, by and large, are the only ones you want to try to get listed on) all search in slightly different ways, and one approach won't work for all of them.

Viral marketing

Viral marketing means marketing that gets your customers spreading the word about your business for you. It is effective and cheap, but it can also be extremely tricky to get going. The most common medium used for viral marketing is e-mails, particularly e-newsletters or bulletins.

If your customers are likely to have e-mail addresses, then it should be a priority for you to try to collect those addresses. E-mail is a brilliantly cost-effective means of communicating with customers. However, if you are collecting e-mail addresses, you will need to follow the procedures under the Data Protection Act to ensure that you are collecting and storing personal information in a responsible way. To find out more, visit the Information Commissioner's site at **www. informationcommissioner.gov.uk**.

Many businesses send e-mail newsletters or bulletins in order to let people know about the latest developments and to promote to existing customers. A good viral marketing campaign can also help bring new customers into the business – for example, by sending out e-mails to customers which they then forward on to their friends, colleagues and families. The most effective viral e-mails either contain some gem of information which can't be found elsewhere, or something funny, topical or quirky. You could offer to give something away for free – 'Send this on to five friends and win a widget', for example. Trying to come up with a brilliant idea for an e-mailer is devilishly difficult to do, but not impossible. Alternatively, you could just strive to make your e-newsletter as well written and engaging as possible so that people read it for pleasure, regardless of whether or not they are actually interested in your business.

A note on spam: whatever you do, don't send e-mails to people who haven't explicitly agreed to receive e-mails from you. Spam is evil and wrong and is the bane of the Internet (this is just our opinion, but we think it will be scientifically proven one day). So only e-mail people who actually want to be e-mailed.

When we were starting out, we found a load of e-mail addresses on one of our family e-mails (someone had forgotten to BCC the e-mail out to everyone). So we thought it might be a good idea to send our newsletter out to all of them, on the off chance that they or someone they knew might be interested in reading it. We learned very quickly that this did not go down well with many recipients. One in fact e-mailed back a reply simply saying 'f**k off'. We hasten to add that it wasn't a close family member. So don't align yourself with the penis extenders, the Viagra sellers, the hot teen promisers and the Nigerian money launderers – steer clear of spam.

Forums and messageboards

If you are looking to promote your business online then you could, as we did, visit various discussion forums or messageboards or chatrooms of relevance and namedrop your business. What you need to look out for is that many forums won't welcome people plugging their own services, so don't rub them up the wrong way by namedropping your business without first checking whether or not it is acceptable.

There are ways and means of broaching the subject which don't sound like an out-and-out advert. For example, if your business sells widgets and you go to the messageboard of *www.widgetownersUK.com* and post a message saying 'check out my brilliant widget site!', then the site administrator will probably take the message down. However, if you post a query or a response to someone else's query and casually mention your site as a secondary thing, you probably won't be thrown off the board.

Running your own messageboard or discussion forum on your website can be a great way to build a community and develop rapport with your customers. However, there is nothing worse than messageboards which have had nothing posted on them for months or a discussion forum with only five members. You need to be confident that you have enough traffic to your site to warrant the creation of a messageboard or forum before setting one up. These kinds of live interactive feature also require a moderator or administrator, or you can end up with all kinds of libel and filth on your website. So remember that you will have to devote time to keeping a regular eye on things. The other thing to bear in mind is that such interaction with your customers can be extremely addictive – and therefore a serious distraction from the rest of your business – so make sure that you genuinely have time to monitor and contribute to forums or messageboards.

Mobile phones

Everyone seems to have a mobile phone nowadays, so being able to market via mobile phones would seem to be a winner. However, it is actually extremely difficult to do. You can obtain your customers' mobile numbers (with their consent, of course) and send them text reminders or messages, but this will only be really relevant for a minority of businesses. There is a general feeling that we are already bombarded with marketing and sales information online and via the TV, radio and printed media, and having such messages coming through on your phone as well could be seen as too intrusive and verging on information overload. Time will tell if this is the case.

CD ROMs and DVDs

These are normally used as promotional items in the same way as a brochure or a website. CD ROMs and DVDs are cheap to duplicate and you can put loads of data on them, including games, video clips, audio clips, sales letters, brochures and virtually anything else that can be stored in digital format. You will have initial design and programming costs to bear, and this kind of media lacks the immediacy of a printed brochure or a website (the user has to actually load it onto their computer which, surprisingly, can be a barrier to them looking at it at all). There is also the impression that people have of CD ROMs and DVDs that, because you can cram so much onto them, they will always take ages to read through. In short, a giveaway CD or DVD will work for some businesses to some customers, but not for others. It's up to you to decide if the initial design and programming costs will pay off in the long run.

TV and radio

Advertising on television and radio is another one of those things that may work for some businesses, but not for others. The plethora of cable channels and radio stations which can now be accessed in your average home or office means that there is certainly a wide choice of media to choose from, but would your business really benefit from it?

The positioning of advertising on TV and radio works in much the same way as advertising in printed media. You need to make sure that the audience is made up of your customers, and that you get your message across effectively. Unless you have lots of initial investment and need to appeal to a mass market, TV advertising on the terrestrial, key satellite and cable channels will be beyond the budgets of most start-ups. So that solves that issue!

We once ran a competition on a local radio station which was aimed at young people – they got listeners ringing up and entering the competition, but we didn't see a sudden rise in hits to our website. This is not to say that radio advertising won't work for your business, but get media packs from local radio stations and find out who listens, when and in what numbers. Listen in yourself to get a feel for whether your company would benefit from being featured.

Wholesalers, agents, brokers and resellers

These all basically act as 'middle men' in the relationship between you and your customers. For example, in the book trade, there are about three or four wholesalers who supply most of the UK's shops with books. So, every now and again, the wholesalers will ring us up, order a number of books from us at a very high discount, then keep them in stock for when bookshops order them. We don't pay them anything, but they make money on our discount. In this particular case you have to use wholesalers, because bookshops don't order directly from the publisher – or at least the big high street chains don't.

Agents work in many different ways depending on the sector they are in. We don't have much to do with agents, apart from estate agents when we are looking for office space (go to Chapter 4 for more on that one). Whether or not an agent could sell your product or service for you totally depends on your business. The same goes for brokers. A broker will normally have a number of products or services from different suppliers to offer customers. They will get a commission or make money on a discount when they make a sale.

Resellers take other people's products or services (usually from more than one supplier) and then sell them on to customers after making money from the suppliers' discount. In the world of educational publishing, there are a number of resellers who send catalogues or sales reps into schools. They then do a sales job on your behalf, but they will also be selling other suppliers' goods too. Some business models work brilliantly on the basis of using middlemen to make their sales. In our particular case, we found that the most effective way for us to sell our products to teachers was by speaking to them directly, but it really does depend on what you are selling and to whom.

Marketing your business effectively may seem like a daunting task and there will be times when you need to ask an expert marketer for advice. However, as long as you understand your product and your customers, and you can communicate with them in a way they understand, you can go a long way by yourself. Most start-ups and SMEs have to deal with their own marketing – they don't have the luxury of employing a specialist.

KELLY MARKS RUNS INTELLIGENT HORSEMANSHIP

I had muddled through life and hit 30 with a love of horses but no money or assets except a car and an eclectic set of skills that were never going to be requested in any job advertisement. An ardent reader of self-help books, I knew 'when the student is ready the teacher will appear' and that's just what happened to me. On 30 April 1993, I met 'The Real Life Horse Whisperer', Monty Roberts, in a petrol station in France. I offered to help him with his autobiography which he'd been trying to put together for eight years. Writing was something I enjoyed and I type fast!

When Monty's book came out, he thought he might do a couple of demonstrations in horsemanship. He'd done them a few years earlier and would get 15 to 50 people attending. Funnily enough, writing adverts was something I'd always had good luck with – a handy thing – and at the first demonstration we were sold out, with 1,000 people attending.

I kept the names and addresses of all the people that came to the first demonstrations and, with a former student who was a bit lost at the time and turned up at my place one evening (who ended up staying two years), wrote to everyone offering weekend and five-day courses. It was just so astonishing/amazing/incredible when the bookings came in! The applications continued to grow in number every year and courses can get fully booked up to seven months in advance. I've never put the price up from those first courses because I always want them to be affordable for as many horse lovers as possible.

Visit Kelly's site at:
www.intelligenthorsemanship.co.uk

PR

Like a popular website, public relations is one of those things that people tend to equate with instant sales success. PR agencies will blind you with science and persuade you of the logic that if three million people read the *Sun*, getting your business featured in the *Sun* means that three million people will then be interested in what you are selling. Bingo! You're a millionaire.

Unfortunately, it doesn't really work like that. As with the Internet, those millions of people reading the *Sun* are not going to read it from cover to cover in minute detail. Some of them will buy it for the TV listings and then throw it away (no offence to the great British institution which is the *Sun* newspaper of course!); many of them won't be interested in reading about your business at all. When we got our first piece of national PR in one of the tabloids with a huge readership, we naturally assumed that at the very least our web hits would shoot up. But no – it had very little noticeable effect. So then we had to think about the odds of someone reading the travel section of a tabloid paper on a particular day, who was interested enough in gap years to pick up the paper and then find a computer to type in our web address and hopefully buy something from our website . . . The odds are definitely not in your favour.

A good PR agent should manage your expectations so that you aren't putting figures in your business plan on the basis of getting lots of PR. For many start-ups, PR is a luxury. Paying wages, rent and the Inland Revenue should be higher on your list of priorities, frankly. But that is not to say that it is a waste of money – it is just difficult to ascribe any tangible benefits to it. Overall though, you can put some general objectives in place which will help your PR plan pay its way.

★ **Positive PR adds kudos to your business. This works in a general sense (people may choose you over another** supplier because your name is familiar or they've read about you in the paper) and in a more direct way, in that you can put 'As featured in the *Daily Echo*' or whatever on your marketing materials.

★ Having a profile in the media does mean that you can make interesting contacts. People will ring up saying 'I read about you in so-and-so', and they may prove to be interesting individuals or work for a business which can help you out.

★ PR which happens repeatedly over a period of time can lead to sales. Being seen as a recognised expert or specialist in your field in the public eye will help your business. However, this will only really sink in if you are featured more than once.

The latter is the reason why having a PR plan is really important. You need to work out what you want to say or do, and when and why. If you have a new product launching, then getting good PR in the relevant press can only be a good thing. To do this effectively though, you need to contact the press then pester them until they actually do something with your press release. This is why using a PR consultant should pay off – it can take up a lot of time and energy badgering journalists into listening to your story.

So a much better idea is to sit down with your PR person and work out a plan. It will need to be a plan that covers at least six months, in order to achieve the coverage that you want and to see any benefits from that coverage. Be absolutely clear on what you want your PR to achieve for you, then work out the best way of going about this.

Think about what you are going to tell which media, and when. Think about your customers and the press they are likely to read, then work out a plan to get your business covered in that press. Research events and exhibitions and decide whether there are going to be any benefits of timing PR around these. Be aware that many publications have very long lead times (for example, a women's glossy monthly magazine will often be looking for interesting features at least three months in advance of the publication date). If you bear in mind these long lead times and the short attention span of journalists and editors, you will be better prepared for the long haul of getting your business PR.

Many publications will read your press release and then try to sell you advertising. This is annoying because if you had wanted to advertise with them, you would have sorted it out already. PR is not a cheap alternative to paid-for advertising – with PR you don't have any choice about where your article is positioned, and if your press release is too sales-focused, the paper or magazine definitely won't be interested in it as a feature. If you are willing to pay for some coverage, it might be worth considering an advertorial which, as the name suggests, is a cross between advertising and editorial. A good advertorial will showcase your products or services, while having a good, interesting 'hook' to the story at the same time. You will normally get more coverage and space with an advertorial than with a straight advert.

The thing to remember with PR is that, as a channel to your market, it is usually pretty hit and miss. Good PR is never a bad thing, but don't rely on it exclusively to raise awareness of your product or services among your target customers. You will need to build it into a marketing plan which includes many other channels.

GET THE BASICS: WRITING A PRESS RELEASE

When your budget allows, you can hire a professional writer to create press releases on your behalf. But you can also do the job yourself, and in the early days this is probably the best option as it's a lot cheaper – and fairly straightforward, if you follow our five-step action plan:

1 Create a good headline

If you want your press release to catch the eye of media editors, you need to make sure that you give it a good headline. This should be the actual headline that you would want to see in print, so make it bold and interesting and ensure that it sounds like a news story and not an advertisement.

For example, 'YORKSHIRE ENTREPRENEURS WIN NATIONAL AWARD' is a news-type headline, and much better than 'YORKSHIRE ENTREPRENEURS WANT YOUR MONEY'.

2 Write a news story

Let's repeat that. Write a *news* story. This means one that is written from a journalist's perspective, as opposed to one that sounds like you are blowing your own trumpet. For example, instead of writing 'We're a brilliant business called XYZ Ltd and we've won several awards', you would write something like 'XYZ Ltd is an innovative business which has won several major awards'. Notice that the former style sounds like a cheesy advertisement and is likely to make you sound arrogant, while the latter sounds like good journalism and creates a healthy sense of respect for your company.

As well as the tone you adopt, it is important to write a news *story*. A press release is much more likely to get published if it actually tells the reader something that is genuinely interesting and newsworthy. Of course, almost anything can be made newsworthy, given the right amount of spin. Having your shop front redecorated could be made newsworthy, if you write about your 'Local Business Remodelling for the Future'. Of course, if you have got something better to write about then you can save the remodelling idea for any dry spell you have in the future!

3 Include your contact details

The aim of a press release is to generate publicity for your business, so always make sure that you include your contact details at the end of the piece. You needn't make a song and dance about this, just include a simple line at the end, such as *XYZ Ltd can be contacted on 01234 567890*.

4 Keep it brief

No print media editor is going to publish a 10,000-word press release which describes your business in painful detail, no matter how newsworthy it is. The prime minister gets a couple of pages, tops, and that's when the scandal-merchants are running the show, so you'll be lucky to get a whole page.

Make things easy for editors by writing a press release which is no more than 750 words or so. If they want more information, they can ask for it. It's always better to err on the side of brevity and have them ask for more words than it is to write a star-studded epic and have them use it as a doorstop.

5 Present it professionally

Presentation matters, and sending a wonderfully-written press release penned in leaky biro on the back of an old envelope will not make the right kind of impression. Instead, adopt professional journalistic standards and present your work in a typewritten font on clean, white A4 paper. Use one side of the paper only and use double spaced lines so that the text is easy on the eyes. The more pleasant the release is to look at, the more chance it has of getting published.

BRANDING

We once talked to a company we were working with about branding. They had recently undergone a major re-branding exercise, which had cost them over £100,000. They had paid that money to an agency to come up with a new identity and name for the business. Let's say, for the sake of confidentiality, that they were originally called Bob Smith Ltd. The day dawned on which their new identity was due to be launched, and the management team awaited the unveiling of the re-branding with great anticipation. The agency revealed the legend – the new company name, which represented the dynamism and growth of the business, was to be . . . Bob Smith Solutions Ltd. And yes, that's a true story.

So what can we learn from that example? Mainly, that as a small business owner, you should try not to worry too much about the name of your business, your company logo or your 'corporate identity'. Obviously your business needs a name, and obviously you will need a logo that doesn't look terrible. But as a start-up, the most important thing is that your product, service and business model are right. Thinking up company names and coming up with brand identities can be among those things which take up much more time than they should.

Think of some of the most successful businesses in the world today – Microsoft, Tesco, Google. If you had lived on a desert island all your life and didn't know what these companies did, you would have no idea that they were hugely successful businesses just by the sound of their names. The name of the business isn't important – it's what the business does that counts.

There is a vast amount of dazzling information out there about branding and the power of brands, but to be honest, you don't want to spend a lot of time or money on getting your brand identity created if you are setting up your own business. Get your business plan right, sort out your suppliers, make sure your website works and get out there to promote your business – all these things are fundamental to your success and therefore much more important than creating a beautiful-looking brand identity. Marketing agencies will hate us for this, but honestly, business is all about making money, and you make money by selling stuff to satisfied customers who like what you do. You could have the worst logo in the world and still be a hugely successful business, and the converse is also true – having a lovely brand identity won't pay the bills.

Once your business is up and running, you can use all the marketing channels at your fingertips to get your brand recognised by as many people as possible, but when you are just starting up you need to stick to the basics.

WRITING YOUR MARKETING PLAN

Once you have considered and understood the various channels to market which you might use to reach your customers, you can start to put your marketing plan together. There is nothing particularly complicated about this – just identify your customers, then identify the ways in which you mean to communicate with them. Assign potential costs and timescales to these ideas, and identify what you want your objectives to be. Make sure that all your marketing objectives link to the overall business objectives. If your business plan says you will be making £100,000 in year one, and this involves selling 100 widgets to 1,000 people, then your marketing plan should show how you plan to communicate to enough people to achieve those 1,000 sales. In general marketing terms, a 5 per cent response rate to a direct mail marketing campaign would be good. So if you want 1,000 sales, you need to get your product or service in front of 20,000 people. Your plan should reflect this. The plan can be as detailed or as complex as you need it to be, and it will all be subject to change anyway – if something isn't working, you will need to judge whether you can afford to keep trying it in the hope it will eventually pay off, or whether you should just knock it on the head.

Your marketing plan is an important part of your overall business plan, so it is vital that you think through all the financial and commercial implications of its success or failure.

TO SUM UP . . .

★ Brainstorm all the different ways in which you can communicate with your customers, then choose the ones that are the most practical and effective.

★ In a marketing plan, identify your customers and how you mean to communicate with them.

★ Always keep your communications simple, direct and accurately written.

★ Don't assume that marketing, PR and design gurus necessarily know what is best for your business when it comes to creating marketing materials and corporate identities. Follow your gut instinct and always do a bit of informal market research by running ideas past friends and family.

★ Don't be afraid to try different approaches to your

customers, but be ready to drop them if they don't work as well as you expect.

★ Don't waste a lot of time coming up with company names and logo ideas.

★ Remember that it is what your business *does* that makes customers come to you – not having a snazzy logo or flashy website.

6

Growing Your Business: Sales

EVERYTHING THAT YOU DO, SAY AND THINK in your business needs to focused around making sales. This is a bitter pill to swallow for many of us who long to run a business, but whose primary motive for doing so is not selling. Unfortunately, selling is an integral part of all businesses and it is a difficult area to get right if it is not something that comes naturally to you.

The good news is that everybody can improve their sales performance. Even if you are the least confident, least outgoing person in the world, you can make sales as long as you are passionate about your product and can identify those people who would be most likely to buy it. Firstly, you will need to stop being the least confident, least outgoing person in the world. Business is no place for shrinking violets. If you aren't happy to tell people about your own business, no-one else will be. But this is easier said than done and confidence isn't just something that you wake up with one morning. The brilliant thing about running your own business, however, is that is gives you scope to develop skills in a way that being an employee does not. There are lots of training and development courses you can go on that will build your selling and communication skills, and you can find out from your local Business Link or Chamber of Commerce whether there is any financial support to help you do this. Read self-help books on communicating, building confidence and selling – the bookshelves are full of them. Practise what you are reading about as well, and commit yourself to attaining certain goals within a certain timescale. These goals might include:

★ Being able to introduce yourself and your business to a group of strangers (within a four-week timescale).
★ Being able to tell a stranger in 30 seconds exactly what your business does (within a two-week timescale).
★ Being able to approach someone you have never met before and introduce yourself (within a four-week timescale).
★ Being able to generate ten new sales leads (potential customers) a week through meetings, phone calls or direct mail (within a two-week timescale).
★ Being able to structure and deliver a sales call to a potential customer (within an eight-week timescale).
★ Being able to close a sale (within an eight-week timescale).

These timescales are just examples. Obviously, the sooner you can build your skills and confidence the better. Work out a plan for each of the goals, breaking it down into manageable chunks. So the first goal, 'Being able to introduce yourself and your business to a group of strangers (within a four-week timescale)', could be broken down into: week 1 – develop your introduction and rehearse it in front of friends and family; week 2 – practise saying it in front of the team at work or a trusted supplier or customer; week 3 – say it to one person you have never met before; week 4 – introduce yourself and your business to a group of strangers.

THE SALES PROCESS

We have already mentioned 'closing' a sale and 'generating leads', but what exactly do these mean? Both are elements of a standard sale process, which can be broken down in the following way:

1 **identify your prospects**
2 **create the opportunity**
3 **pitch**
4 **close**
5 **deliver**
6 **follow up**

Firstly, you need to identify your prospects, or who your potential customers are. If we use the example of someone selling dog brushes, they would need to find a load of people who might be interested in buying those brushes. The obvious target would be dog owners. So you would identify your channels to this market and gradually build a number of prospects. Let's say you identify the owner of a pet shop, who specialises in dog-grooming accessories, as a potential customer. He is a prospect. The first thing you need to do is your research. Find out as much as you can about his business and what he does. Have a good snoop around his shop before you identify him as a prospect even, and find out what he is already doing within your remit and how you may be able to improve on this.

You now need to create the sales opportunity. You decide to do this by calling the pet shop owner. At this stage you need to work on the initial part of your sales pitch, and the first thing you should ask him is not 'Do you want to buy my dog brushes?' but 'Could you tell me about the dog-grooming products you have in stock?'. This is an open question, inviting the prospect to talk. In any initial call like this, the majority of your time should be spent listening to what the prospect is telling you in response to your open question. In this way you understand the prospect's needs and start to build a relationship with him. The prospect thinks that your primary motivation isn't to sell him your dog brushes, but to find out if he is happy with his present supply. If he isn't, then you are offering him a solution.

The pitch is when you come in with the benefits of your dog brushes over every other dog brush on the market. It sounds like we are stating the obvious, but it is vital to know your own product or service inside out before getting to this stage. You need to be able to match customer needs with your own offering. Focus on the benefits of what you are offering, rather than the features. So instead of saying 'These dog brushes have extra strong combing bristles with dogswelox', you say 'These brushes relax the dog and make for an enjoyable owner/pet experience' (or something along those lines). Focus on matching the benefits of your product to the needs of your customer, based on the conversation you have already have with him.

Closing a sale effectively is one of the hardest things to do for someone who is inexperienced at sales. The easiest way of doing this is by getting the customer to buy in to minor features of your offering throughout the pitch process. So in the dog brush example, you could ask at specific stages questions like 'these bristles are made of solid dogswelox, meaning that the dog instantly relaxes when groomed. This would be a great benefit to your customers wouldn't it?', or 'the dog hairs fall out of these brushes incredibly easily, which would really make an owner's life a lot easier when cleaning the brushes wouldn't it?' What you want them to say is lots of little 'yeses' in the run up to the big 'Yes!' when you ask them if they would like now to place an order. There are various ways of doing this. Some are tactful: 'So, that is our range in full. Would you now like to talk about discounts on larger orders?'; others are more in your face: 'Shall we move on with this together?' You need to find a style that suits you and your product or service, but that also gets a signed order form from the customer, or cash changing hands. Always be 100 per cent clear about any order the customer is making – have written order forms with prices, quantities, terms and conditions and discounts to hand, or clarify in writing that the customer would like to go ahead with the order, on what terms and in what quantities.

Make sure that the customer understands when the product or service can be delivered, and that it is convenient with them. If necessary, get a deposit upfront. If you are offering an ongoing service, establish how payments will be made and on what timescale. At this point the customer has to be 100 per cent committed to the sale.

Once you have said when the product or service will be delivered, stick to your promise. If something happens which means you can't, get on the phone and explain. Make sure the delivery is prompt and is to the right address. Get the customer's name and contact details right on all the documentation which accompanies the order.

Once delivery has been made, follow up at regular intervals with communications to your customers. Ask often if everything is alright with them, if they are pleased with their purchase. If anything is wrong, sort it out straight away. See a successful sale as the beginning of a long and happy relationship with your customer, not as an end in itself.

Because the owner of a small business or start-up is so closely identified with the business itself in the eyes of customers, you have to come to terms with the fact that, as much as selling your products or services, you are selling yourself. We don't mean this in any derogatory way – it is just that even when prospects love what you do or what you produce, if they don't like or have faith in you as an individual, they won't buy. This is where a really strong brand is usually handy. When you walk into TopShop, you are going in because you like the brand, not because you like Philip Green. However, very few small businesses have a brand with this much impact and your prospects will be sold on you, as much as on your product or service.

HOW TO WIN PROSPECTS AND INFLUENCE PEOPLE

The realisation that not only will you need to communicate to strangers and sell them something, but make them like you as well, can be enough to put people off setting up their own business. But don't panic. This is a brilliant opportunity to find out what you are really capable of achieving. We have already mentioned elsewhere in this book how great running your own business is in terms of personal development. To make people really want to work with you, you have to make them like you. And human beings tend to like people who are a bit like them. We're not suggesting that you become a human chameleon and spend your life developing multiple personalities, but you do need to learn to gauge the psychological make-up of others quickly and accurately before pitching to them. Developing this kind of perception and empathy can help you in all areas of your life, not just in business.

For example, put yourself in the shoes of a buyer. You want to buy some jewellery from a bespoke designer. You have meetings booked in with three designers. You are open minded about the sort of thing that you want to buy, so are looking forward to having some suggestions put your way. From what you have seen, you like the designs of all three candidates equally, and you have a budget of £50.

The first designer comes in and shows you her portfolio. She is wearing a long vintage skirt and a home-made cardigan. She is very quietly spoken, mumbles when asked questions, avoids eye contact and seems very shy. She apologises for the fact that her portfolio is a bit disorganised. She says she thinks she could make the sort of thing you want for £25. When you say you will think about it, she looks a bit tearful.

The second designer comes in and runs through his design ideas on a PowerPoint presentation, which he flicks through so quickly you can't read it properly. He is wearing a turquoise suit and very shiny shoes. He talks very quickly and you find yourself trying to get a word in edgeways. He makes lots of eye contact and smiles frequently. His last words to you are 'So what sort of thing are you after?' You finally get the chance to explain and he says he can do it for £45, but he needs payment up-front.

The third designer comes in and is wearing a dress rather like one that you own. She makes eye contact, smiles and asks you what you are looking for exactly. When you say you don't want anything too kitsch, she nods and says that she dislikes kitsch jewellery too, although kitsch does have its place in her record collection. You own up to having the entire ABBA back catalogue. She laughs and says that her favourite ABBA song is

'Chiquitita'. You love that one too . . . She says that it is too early to say exactly how much the sort of item you are looking for would cost, as she would need show you the range of materials that are available first, but it will be at least £50. This will be payable in instalments, at pre-determined stages of the design process.

Which of the designers would you want to design your jewellery?

As a customer, you need to have faith that the person you are buying something from is personally capable of delivering it. If that person is barely capable of making eye contact, you will doubt their ability to do anything else. You also need to trust them as a person not to rip you off. If they are talking money and payment up-front without any real understanding of what it is that you are looking for, you will doubt their trustworthiness. Finally, you need to be able to respect them as an individual, and it is much easier to respect people who have demonstrated that they are thoughtful, honest and who have given an impression that they are rather like you.

To get to the stage of being able to pitch effectively to people, you don't have to be like one of the salespeople on a home shopping channel. What they are doing is selling without any input from the customer at all. It is a full-on sales pitch, showing all the features and some of the benefits of the products. This is fine if you are selling saucepans on TV, but not if you are trying to get your customers to have genuine faith in your ability to deliver, trust you to treat them fairly and respect you as an individual. So don't worry about getting your sales patter right – learn to ask the right questions, to listen to the answers, to identify with the customer on a personal level, to know your product and your customer inside out, and then align the customer's needs with the benefits of the product or service you are going to sell – or that you hope you will sell!

In the example we used above, the reason that the pitch of the third jeweller sounded good was because she had picked up on something which you and she had in common (i.e. a love of kitsch 70s disco). Being able to find commonalities between people is a very valuable skill to have, and is essential when you are running your own business. You have to understand your customers and what they have in common, what makes them different, and how you and your business can relate to all those things. This is particularly true if you are very different from those people you are selling to. For instance, if you are 22 years old and knitting jumpers for golf-playing retirees, you will need to work that little bit harder to find the commonalities between yourself and your customers. It could be that you are as passionate about golf and keeping warm as they are. That would be enough to begin with.

DECISION-MAKERS

If you are having to cold-call prospects without knowing their organisation very well, you could waste a great deal of time speaking to secretaries, PAs and more junior people in the organisation before you get to speak to the person you really need to reach . . . if you can get to speak to them at all, that is. This is particularly the case if you are intent on telling people about how wonderful you are, rather than listening to what they are telling you. You could, for example, waste ten minutes pitching to a prospect on the phone, when if you had only let them talk about their own role in the first place, you would have realised that they were not the appropriate person to talk to. You could have then asked them who would be the right lead. The best way of avoiding this is by being completely straight up about who you need to speak to. Clarify early on in the conversation whether or not the person you are speaking to is the one with the buying power. If so, great. If not, ask who would be the right person to speak to – after all you don't want to waste anybody's time.

If the person you need to speak to is relatively high up the organisation and unlikely to take cold calls, be persistent. Get her e-mail address (which is given out more easily than direct phone lines, in some cases) and send an e-mail outlining what you would like to discuss. (Remember to couch this in terms of her business requirements, rather than what you have to sell her – so instead of 'I've got some brilliant widgets to make your life much easier', say 'as the number one supplier of widget-based technology, I understand that you are always looking for ways to improve your service . . .') Then you need to call and call and call until either you get a response, or you get told to go away and not bother her again. Ideally, rather than being told to go away, you should get to the point where you can say 'OK, I understand at this point you are happy with your existing widget supplier. Can I drop you an e-mail or call you in the future to keep up to date with any developments?' If she says yes, then keep in touch with her every month or so, always being positive, always being helpful, always looking for feedback.

Pester power is enormously helpful when you are trying to get someone's attention. There is a fine line between being persistent and being annoying, but by staying on the right side of that fine line you are more likely to reach the person you need to speak to. The bottom line is this: unless you get out there and start talking to people about what you do and converting those conversations into cash, you will never make any money. Sales are the *raison d'être* for a business, and in most cases, as the owner/manager, you are the person to make them happen.

NETWORKING FAQs

Networking events can be helpful for start-up businesses. Below we have listed some frequently asked questions about networking which will help you to ensure that your networking is effective.

Why should I bother with networking?

It all depends on your business objectives and the type of business you are running. If you need to make a certain amount of sales and you are offering a service to other businesses, then networking could be an opportunity to source sales leads. Conversely, if you are looking for help with accountancy or HR, you could meet helpful accountants or HR specialists at networking events. Networking can also help you to find out more about your sector, or about specific business issues. The more specific you can be about your reasons for attending networking events, the better (although probably everyone has attended events just because there is free food and drink available at some point in their business lives!).

What kind of network events are there available?

Obviously it will depend on where you are located, but usually the following organisations will be good sources of information on networking:

★ Business Link – **www.businesslink.gov.uk**
★ your Regional Development Agency – **www.consumer.gov.uk/rda/info**

★ **your local Chamber of Commerce –
www.chamberonline.co.uk**

You can also find websites and phone numbers for to other networking organisations in the 'Useful Links' section of this book.

Does it cost money to attend these events?
It depends on the organisation. Generally speaking, though, it shouldn't cost a lot to get involved.

What time are networking events held?
It varies. Some events are breakfast events (which are a no-no if you have to drop kids off at school or sort them out in the morning – event organisers take note). Others are lunch-time or evening affairs.

Which ones will work best for me?
Ask yourself what, ideally, you want to get from attending networking events. Have clear goals in your mind when you go. There is absolutely no point in saying 'I am going to go and force myself to speak to five people' just for the sake of it (although, if you are nervous at these kind of events, this might actually be good practice). If you are attending networking events to get new business, then find out as much as you can about the profile of the other attendees. If you are attending to find out about something specific, make sure it will be on the agenda. If you just want to go and meet new people in the same industry as yourself for a bit of moral support, then identify a networking event which is industry specific.

How do I network effectively?

Entering a room full of strangers can be a daunting experience. If you are going to a networking event on your own, make sure you go equipped with the following:

★ business cards
★ some practised intros – even if it just saying 'Hi I'm XXX, what do you do?'
★ your elevator pitch
★ three positive things to tell people about your business
★ a smile

The last two may seem odd things to include, but they are key to successful networking. A smile is the single best way of breaking the ice and communicating with people who you don't know. It invites communication – think about it, if you are in a room full of people and someone nearby smiles at you and makes eye contact, how likely would you be to walk away from them? You would almost certainly make the effort to speak to them.

To make the most of a networking event, you will need to listen to what other people are saying as well as speaking yourself. By listening carefully to what people are telling you, you can respond appropriately and decide whether or not there is mutual benefit in the conversation going forward.

If you find it very hard to walk up to strangers and make conversation, then ask the network organiser if they can introduce you to someone who may be of relevance to you. Any organiser worth their salt will have a good idea of the make up of their attendees and will know good people for you to meet. Whatever you do, don't just walk into a room, make a beeline for the drinks or food and stand in a corner like a wallflower. Force yourself to smile, make eye contact and use your practised intros.

The reason we recommend remembering three positive things about your business is that there is nothing more off-putting than speaking to someone at a networking event who is negative or apologetic about what they do. It's amazing how many times you meet people, ask them what they do, and they come back with 'Tree surgeon, for my sins', or 'Lawyer – yes I know, I'm sorry too'. Thinking of positive things to say about your business means that you are prepared for common questions like 'What's that like?', or 'That must be interesting?'. So instead of rolling your eyes and launching into a ten-minute statement about the horrors of running your own business, you should be able to recite all the positive things which will keep the listener's interest.

How can I get people to remember me after the event?

Human beings are very predictable when it comes to what sticks in their mind about other people. Visual triggers are an obvious way to get people to remember you. Wear something that makes you stand out from the crowd – it doesn't need to be a clown outfit or a pair of bunny ears. Remember that you will be talking to people relatively close up, so you can wear a piece of unusual jewellery or an accessory that will act as a discussion point and as a visual trigger. You will then often find, when making follow-up phone calls later on, you can jog people's memories immediately, simply by saying 'I was the lady with the pink scarf', or 'I was wearing the big silver brooch'. Ideally, of course, you want people to remember you for your fascinating discussion, but this isn't always possible at events which can be busy or noisy.

How can I make sure that my time spent networking is of benefit to my business?

This is a key question. There is no point in going to networking events for the sake of it, which is why you have to think about your objectives in advance. Some businesses don't need networking events at all, which is fine. Others will benefit from attending, but only if they are sure they are attending the right events for the right reasons. As with most things, effective networking will be more likely to happen if you have a plan:

★ Research the event – who will be there, who do you want to speak to and why? Speak to the organisers to find out more if necessary.

★ Prepare yourself with the things on the list above (ears, smile, business cards etc) and book yourself in.

★ When you get there, there may be a welcome desk with name badges on it. Have a good scan through the badges or the attendance list if you get a chance to double-check on who they are expecting there.

★ Network, network, network! Don't forget to collect business cards from people you are interested in, and make sure you give yours out.

★ Follow up any leads or interesting conversations with a friendly phone call no more than two days after the event.

★ Enter all contacts into a written or computer database or address book.

Networking can be a valuable benefit for your business, but only if you make a good job of it and if it is targeted in terms of what you want to get out of it. It can be a big distraction if you are intent on going to every event that crops up, so keep focused on your business objectives and how some selective networking could help you attain these.

TO SUM UP . . .

★ Without sales, you have no business, no matter how brilliant your idea is.

★ You can become a perfectly good salesperson.

★ Set yourself goals.

★ Think of it as a learning opportunity.

★ Develop a clear sales process.

★ Listen to your customers.

★ Do your research.

★ Learn to close the sale effectively.

★ Think of a sale as the beginning of a relationship, rather than the end of a transaction.

★ Identify the decision-maker and be persistent and consistent in your communications with him or her.

★ If you are using networking as a source of sales leads, be specific in terms of who you want to contact and why at each event.

7

Your Business and You

THE RELATIONSHIP BETWEEN A BUSINESS and its owner/ manager is often complicated. When you start a business, you feel in control. You are setting it up, deciding on direction and how much time you want to spend on it. Before you know it, however, the business starts to take on a life of its own – and you run the risk of the business controlling you rather than vice versa. It is never nice feeling that you are not in control, so you have to learn to manage your time and resources really effectively to prevent your business taking over your life. This is more the case for people running their own businesses than those who are employed by other people. Owner/managers take their work home with them far more frequently than employees do.

Of course, ideally, your work is something you love so much that you don't mind the time it takes up. In reality, however, there are other things in your life which make demands on your time – including family, hobbies and general life management stuff. Things change over time as well; when you start out, the buzz of setting up something which is new and exciting will keep you going through nights, weekends and supposed holidays. When the honeymoon period wears off, however, and you find yourself dealing with all sorts of things which weren't in your original plan (like arguing with suppliers, managing staff, filling in forms, dealing with red tape and producing figures for the bank manager), you may start to resent your business encroaching on your home life.

BALANCING BUSINESS AND KIDS

Women have babies. It's a fact. Women generally have most of the childcare responsibilities. That's also a fact. There is not a lot you can do about the fact that you are female and that you can give birth. You can of course choose not to have a family, but many women want to be able to have a career and children. Setting up your own business does mean that you can work and earn money on your own terms to an extent, but you should never underestimate how much time and commitment you need to get a business up and running. Going it alone isn't always the easiest option.

There are always compromises and difficult decisions that need to be made when it comes to balancing business and kids, especially when it comes to having a new baby. When you are working for an employer, you can ask for months off on maternity leave. When it is your own business though, you will always have to allocate some of your time off to your business – you can't just leave it to run itself. You will be lucky if you're not juggling nappies with sales within the first few weeks after the birth! Your partner can help out, of course, but many couples can't afford to take much unpaid paternity leave, and as a mum you will want to spend a lot of time with a new baby.

As with all things, it is important to set the expectations of everybody involved before you go on maternity leave. If you employ staff, let them know how long you will be on leave for and how available you are going to be during that time. Let them know what your priorities are and what you do and don't need or want to be contacted about. If you will be popping in for update meetings, let them know when they will be and what you want to know in each one. Run through your list of contacts and mark out anyone who you will take direct calls from in the weeks immediately after giving birth.

For your customers and clients, you will need to let them know when your maternity leave begins, how long you will be away for, who they can contact in your absence, what the best means of contact is while you are on leave and whether you will be coming back, full or part time.

Check with an accountant that there is nothing that needs filing at Companies House or HM Revenue & Customs while you are on leave and that your accounts won't be abandoned. You will need to plan from a financial point of view for your maternity leave – how much time can you afford to take off, and can the business pay its bills when you aren't working?

Talk to your partner and your family about what your plans are for maternity leave and about what the implications are from a childcare point of view when you return to work.

REBECCA SAYS:

When we started Gapwork, my daughter was about a year old and I didn't want to spend the whole working week away from her. Kirsty and I agreed that we needed to work 40 hours a week each, so I worked for three days in the office and made up the remainder by working evenings and through the weekends. This worked well at that time, as I was having to speak to contacts in Australia and New Zealand as part of the research for the books and website, and the time difference meant that I had to work weird hours anyway. As time went on, I got a bit older, had a second baby and just lost the ability to work late at night; at weekends the only thing I wanted to do was to chill out with my family and collapse into bed of an evening. It was still important to both Kirsty and myself that we worked equal hours, so I chose to come back to work full time, but have evenings and weekends completely free – and make the most of my holiday time. When you have children, childcare can make a massive difference to your ability to commit enough time to your business. With my first daughter, I was able to work on certain days and at certain times, as she was in a day nursery. Since my second daughter was born, I have had a full-time childminder who only works with my children, from my house. This means that there is no mad rush to drop the kids off at nursery in the morning, and that they get out and about with their carer. This has made my working life a lot easier, but it's important to find a solution which is right for *you* and *your* family, especially when you have children who are pre-school age.

When it comes to setting up your own business, the key to a successful work/life balance is to make sure that you are being realistic in terms of how much time you can dedicate to your work. One absolutely sure-fire recipe for stress is trying to combine looking after kids with your job (unless, of course, looking after kids *is* your job, which is a realistic solution for some women). The very thought of talking business on the phone or trying to work on the computer while the kids are careering around the house dressed as Princess-Space-Barbie armed with yoghurt and felt-tip pens is enough to make Rebecca break out in a cold sweat. She knows that work and home should function together holistically, but for the sake of her sanity, she has had to learn how to switch on and off. It's also horribly unfair to the children to be giving them a fraction of your attention when you are at home. If Rebecca finds herself feeling strung out and telling the kids 'not now!', or 'in a minute', or 'give me a second' all the time, she knows that she has to get some help with the house or look again at her workload.

JILL JOHNSON RUNS TWINKLES NURSERIES

Developing an effective work-life balance is a never-ending challenge and the goalposts move constantly. When you work full time running two businesses as well as having young children, your thinking time is generally non existent. When you do find time to think, generally it consists of feeling guilty about where your children are, whether they are OK, or that you don't spend enough quality time with them. However, I am adamant about having a career – I need a challenge.

My husband, Johnny, was working 60 hours a week all over the country and I was teaching full time when I fell pregnant with Beth, who is now 6. I decided that I would go back to work part time once she was born and agreed to work three days a week. However, I found the job less enjoyable because although my role remained the same, the hours I worked had changed and I ended up working late into the night, every night, to keep up with the workload.

Eventually I decided to take a career break and spend some time with Beth, tendering my resignation in May 2001, finishing at the end of July 2001.

In the meantime, I began setting up the nursery business with a partner, as neither of us could find good childcare in the local area. This not only enabled me to be around my child all day every day, but also to have a hand in her early years' education and care. It also gave her an added sense of security.

The first nursery opened in September 2001, and my daughter attended three days a week (to start with, the two directors' children were the only ones attending). Soon the numbers built – along with the workload. My son, Leo, was born in December 2002, after a very difficult pregnancy. I had 12 weeks' maternity leave which was hard, but I still managed to run two payrolls in between changing nappies during this time. Leo attended the nursery from when he was 12 weeks old, for three days a week. Again, it has given me great pleasure to understand and have a hand in his care and education.

Although you are constantly on call 24 hours a day when you run your own business (and I can work often at night once the children have gone to bed), I try to work four days a week, having Fridays with Leo – and Beth, until she went to school. I always have at least two hours of quality time with the children in the evening before putting them to bed. We make time to bake, eat tea together, read, do homework, have a bath or have friends over to play. Sundays are family days, when we plan to do special things together.

I also mustn't forget that I am very lucky to have family support from both sets of grandparents, who care for the children during school holidays and do school pick ups etc for me. Both my children have thoroughly enjoyed spending a day a week with their grandma.

My family knew I was not fully satisfied in my previous job. They were incredibly supportive of my decision not only to throw them into a degree of chaos, but also to increase our vulnerability. As with many new ventures, our house was – and still is – on the line because of the heavy bank borrowing which I used to fund the business. However well you plan, in service-based businesses where each fee earner can only see one client at a time (i.e. no product which has the potential to be sold to millions!), the first few years are tough and it is a test of holding your nerve and rapidly learning to adapt and change. There is no time for ignoring things that are not working and there is no choice but to put in the hours to get the business off the ground. As for family, I can honestly say that I am glad I did not do this when my children were younger: huge amounts of time and focus are needed for the early years of a business. I am very lucky that my two sons are busy in their own right now, so they have not missed me as they might have done had they been younger. My husband is a workaholic as well, so if anything he respects and expects my commitment to the business. Would I do it again? One hundred per cent, yes!

Visit Balanced Being online at:
www.balancedbeing.com

BALANCING WORK TIME AND PERSONAL TIME

Setting up a business can have a negative impact on your relationship with your partner and your family. If your partner doesn't share your passion for the business or understand your motives for wanting to do it, your work can easily become a bone of contention in the home. If you are in a relationship, then it is really important to talk to your partner about the implications of you setting up a business before you actually start doing it. Through these discussions, you should explore all the possible impacts on your life together. Ask the following questions:

★ What are the benefits of setting up your own business going to be? (These could include giving you something to do, allowing you more freedom in terms of your working hours, making lots of money.)

★ How much money do you need to set it up and where will it come from?

★ What might happen if it all goes wrong? (Will you lose a lot of money? Could you lose your family home? Can you survive on one person's income?)

★ How much time is your business going to take up? (Be realistic.)

★ What hours will you need to work and how much impact will this have on your home life?

One of the main bugbears of women who work is that they are still expected to do the housework and to run the house by the rest of their family. This is particularly annoying when you are setting up your own business, as you will almost certainly be working all hours trying to fit in everything that you need to do. The last thing that you want is to spend all day trying to set up your business, come home, make dinner and then be faced with an evening of tidying up. It sounds really petty, but housework can actually become a real vampire of your time and cause bad feeling between yourself, your partner and any kids. The only way you can avoid this is either to split the labour equally between everyone in the house who is old enough to tidy up after themselves, or to pay for a cleaner. If you are able to run your business on a part-time basis, you may have the time to cook and clean as well as spend quality time with your family and friends – but most start-ups will require your undivided attention, and you will need to start prioritising your time.

So discuss your plans with your partner, if you have one, and make it clear to everyone who shares your home with that you need their practical help around the house so that you are able to spend quality time with them.

When you are in the midst of setting up your business, you may find that your relationship with your partner suffers because you aren't around as much, and when you are, you are distracted by phone calls and e-mails from work. To prevent either of you feeling neglected or unloved, it is important to be honest about what is happening and to find time to spend together. Otherwise you can become so wrapped up in what is going on at work that one day you turn around and realise that you haven't got a relationship with your partner left at all. Sometimes it is nice just to be able to crash out together on the sofa in front of the TV, but try to make your quality time work better for you by doing something that means you actually talk to each other and that you make a bit of an effort. Cooking and eating a meal together at home is always a good way of catching up and sharing time in an enjoyable way – although to make it really work, you should turn off mobile phones and put the landline onto answer phone. Ban the TV and the Internet for the evening and if you've got kids, make sure they are in bed or out of the way. As we mentioned earlier, if your house is a mess and you've got piles of laundry to do, you will find it hard to switch off – so if possible make sure that the chores have been sorted out by other people so that you aren't clock-watching through the meal.

If you don't go out much with your partner, or if you have different groups of friends, try making dates to go out together. Again, it is all about spending proper quality time doing stuff that is different from work or kids or whatever else you have going on in your life. It is easy to take people for granted when you are constantly having to run around for work, and you need to take time out to remind yourselves that you do actually really enjoy each other's company. If you can afford it (and can sort out childcare if necessary), try some weekend breaks together. You don't have to go abroad – there are loads of fantastic getaways in the UK which make the weekends more time effective. If your work is really hectic, try just changing down a gear for the weekend. Don't do anything. Don't schedule anything in. Experiment with being bored. Whatever you do, don't dabble in any work. Potter in the garden, walk to the park, pretend the outside world doesn't exist. Spend the whole weekend in bed, if you are lucky enough to be able to do so without having the neighbours call social services about the feral children smashing up the house. Think of this as downtime when your brain can have a rest.

One thing to remember is that, while working for financial security and being able to afford nice things is all very well, if your relationships are suffering as a result of the amount of time you are spending at work, there is something wrong. Setting up your own business should be a liberating experience which enables you to feel *more* in control of your life, not less. So when you are deciding what kind of business you want to run and your reasons for doing it, be completely honest about how much time and energy you want, or are able, to devote to it.

It's also important to remember that, besides keeping your

close personal relationships going and running your business, there are all the other things that you need to stay on top of – making sure the bills are paid on time, taking care of yourself and your family's health, having a social life, having hobbies or taking part in sporting activities, and generally being a fully-rounded functioning human being, rather than a work-obsessed freak.

BALANCING YOUR BUSINESS AND YOUR HEALTH

This may seem like an afterthought, but looking after yourself when you are running your own business is vital. After all, if you allow yourself to get run down or stressed out, it is your business that will suffer. In the case of most SMEs, if you as the owner/manager have to go off sick, then the business simply won't function.

Running your own business isn't a walk in the park. You are responsible for making decisions, for making sales and – if you have staff – for the livelihoods of other people. If your products or services aren't right, then your customers or clients could suffer, and they will definitely complain. The stress of running your own business is the payback for the freedom and control that it gives you. On the one hand you don't have to report to a useless boss, on the other hand you have little real support when it comes to the crunch. The question you have to ask yourself is 'Am I able to shoulder this much responsibility?' And the only way you'll really know is when you have a go. It's when you are in the midst of it that you realise how much responsibility you have taken on and how little support there really is for owner/managers. This is what leads to stress.

The Health & Safety Executive (**www.hse.gov.uk**) has produced Management Standards for identifying and dealing with employee stress. The Management Standards identify six key areas of work that, if not properly managed, can lead to stress. These six areas are:

★ demands
★ control
★ support
★ relationships
★ role
★ change

It is interesting to look at how each of these areas can make an owner/manager's life more stressful.

★ **Demands.** According to a survey by the Employment Law Advisory Service, one in three small business owners works more than 48 hours per week, which is the current limit set by the European Working Time Directive. As an owner/manager you often have to deal with demands which in larger organisations would be spread between different departments. You will also have to deal with customer queries or strategic planning, often outside normal office hours.

★ **Control.** This is one area which theoretically should be better for an owner/manager than an employee, as you should be in control of what you are doing. In reality though, the temptation to take too much on at once can lead to even the most go-getting entrepreneur feeling as if their workload is out of control.

★ **Support.** You really need the support of your family and friends if you are going to run a business successfully. No woman is an island, and if you have no-one to turn to when things get tough or you need advice, you will feel isolated and stressed. You also need the support of your employees, if you have them, but be aware that it is very hard for staff to put themselves in your shoes and really sympathise; they are often too wrapped up in their own tasks. Employees have trade unions and all sorts of organisational support when things aren't going well at work. They get time off sick (usually paid) and if the worst comes to the worst, they can resign. Owner/managers can't resign without losing the business.

★ **Relationships.** Good relationships at home and in the workplace are important for everyone. If you dread facing your staff or find them a constant source of conflict and aggravation, there is something badly wrong. Your employees have to trust and respect you, as well as like you, to have a good working relationship. The temptation is to try to be 'one of the gang', but remember David Brent in 'The Office' – no-one respects a boss who desperately tries to be best mates with their staff.

★ **Role.** If you started your business as a passionate baker, your role was clearly marked out. You baked bread, it made you happy, you were good at it, your customers liked it and you sold lots. To satisfy demand, you then had to take on some apprentice bakers and some shop staff. Before you know it, you don't have time to be a baker any more – you are a manager, a financial director and an HR consultant. Your role has changed as the business has grown. To be truly happy in what you are doing, you need to be happy with your role and be aware of when it is changing. If you are OK with this, fine. If not, you need to think again.

★ **Change.** Change stresses out your average person. Humans like stability and knowing what is in store for them every day. As an entrepreneurial owner/manager, however, you must be aware that change is par for the course. To succeed in business, you have to be able to adapt to change and respond quickly when circumstances around you alter. Your ability to cope with change will be tested to the full when you are running your own business, but as long as you are prepared for this, you should be able to cope. What might be more stressful is people at home reacting badly to the changes which your entrepreneurial vision has introduced to their lives, and your employees reacting badly to your decisions when dealing with change.

In short, if you think it is stressful working for someone else, you should try running your own business. The good news is that it is a different kind of stress – because you are more in control and better prepared for change, you don't feel as if you are being forced to cope with someone else's problems. They may be problems, but at least they are your problems.

MANAGE YOUR TIME

Dealing with stress is vital when running your own business, and the key is getting on top of your time management. Do a bit of a time audit and work out how much time you currently dedicate to the following:

★ your partner (if you have one)
★ your kids (if you have them)
★ other family responsibilities
★ work
★ travelling (not holidays!)
★ sleeping
★ eating
★ exercise
★ hobbies
★ social life
★ housework

If you are up at 7 am and go to bed at 10 pm, your waking hours are 15 per day. A usual working day is eight hours, which leaves seven for everything else. Factor in two hours for eating and cooking and you have five hours left. If you are lucky, you will only spend an hour travelling to and from work. That leaves four hours per day to devote to your partner, kids, family, friends, exercise, hobbies, social life and housework. Something will clearly have to give. In many cases this will be a social life, hobbies and exercise, as housework unfortunately has to be done to some extent, even if it only involves putting a load of laundry in and stacking the dishwasher.

But by prioritising in this way, you are using all your time to do stuff which expends your energy. Work, family (bless 'em), travelling and housework are all things which use up your energy, and you are spending all of your time on these things. Even sleeping and eating become something which you have to do, rather than something which you relax and enjoy. Eating is often rushed and disjointed, sleep is irregular and broken, and before you know it you aren't investing any quality time in your physical or psychological wellbeing. This is the point at which stress really kicks in and you begin to function well below par. This will have a direct impact on your business and your staff. Customers and clients won't trust you as you seem exhausted, forgetful and make some bad decisions. You become snappy and short tempered, and worst of all you start to take out your stress on those closest to you, so that time spent with your family isn't pleasurable.

The solution here is to re-prioritise your time. The obvious (and most difficult) thing to reduce how long you are spending at work. Do this by delegating tasks to other people, planning your day and your tasks more effectively, and reducing time spent on anything which isn't absolutely crucial to the success of your business. 'No' is a very useful word to bandy around. Practise saying it to the following requests:

★ 'Do you know where my trousers/PE Kit/keys are?' – NO (what this question actually means is 'can you find them for me?')
★ 'Can you pick up my dry cleaning?' – NO
★ 'Can you cook a meal for ten at the weekend?' – NO
★ 'Will you post these for me?' – NO
★ 'Can you sort this out for me?' – NO
★ 'Can you write this up for me?' – NO

You get the idea. 'No' is actually a very liberating word. Use it wisely and you will soon find that people get the message and demands made on your time by those who essentially can't be bothered to do things themselves start to dwindle. It is human nature to want to be helpful (particularly if you happen to be female), but cave women didn't run their own businesses, contribute to the economy, employ people and have big piles of ironing to contend with.

Learn to say 'no' to requests for your time if they aren't going to be of direct benefit to your business (or if you can't see how they will be of benefit). Reclaim some of your time from the grasp of your business and associated people. Identify those people at work who monopolise your time and keep meetings to a minimum. Work with meeting agendas which are distributed beforehand, and cap meeting times. In our experience, it is rare that a meeting has any real benefits after running for an hour. Be ruthless with e-mails and delete everything that isn't relevant to what you are doing.

All of these can be short-term measures so that eventually you can get your head above water and get on top of things again. But you may find that actually these things are useful as ongoing rules.

YOUR PERSONAL WELLBEING ACCOUNT

Once you have freed up some time, even if it is just one hour per day, spend it doing something which is a deposit in your personal wellbeing account. Whether it is taking an hour at lunch to exercise, or get a massage, or read a book somewhere quiet, or catch up with friends, think of something to do that will allow you to genuinely chill out. Avoid the temptation to eat junk food, drink alcohol, have a fag break, watch daytime TV or do something which actually has detrimental effects on your health or psyche. Time is a precious commodity, and it is easy to waste it in our hectic world of information overload and consumerism. A mum will automatically think 'If I'm not at work then I should be at home with the kids', but that isn't the point of this exercise. Taking one hour out a day to do something which places no demands on you whatsoever but makes you feel happier will make the time you do spend with your kids more enjoyable.

Resign yourself to the fact that when you are running your business, you will never be bored for lack of something to do. A business will always have more stuff that could be done to it. The job is never finished, even when it is hugely successful. In fact, when it is hugely successful there will be even more opportunities that could be taken advantage of. If you understand this from the beginning, then you won't feel bitter about your business taking up so much of your time, and you won't spend every waking hour stressing about everything that you could be doing at work.

You probably don't want to spend less time with your loved ones, so you can leave them their time chunk, or think about increasing it (as long as it doesn't start to impinge on your investment time). We've discussed the housework issue already – and unless you genuinely love doing housework, the time you spend on this needs to be firmly controlled. If you have a choice between catching up with the ironing or going for a swim, which do you do? The ironing can wait. No-one has ever died (to our knowledge) because they wore a creased shirt. On the other hand, your physical and psychological wellbeing are actually a matter of life and death.

Travelling to and from work can take a huge amount of time, and one of the main benefits of running your own business is that you can choose to work nearer to home. We have always had this as a criterion, partly because neither of us like driving very much and partly because we object to dealing with rush-hour traffic. Working for yourself does mean that, to an extent, you can choose your working hours and avoid the rush hour. When you are choosing premises, or indeed deciding on what kind of business you want to run, think about how the travelling element may affect your work/life balance. Ideally you want to be able to start and finish every day with the minimum of external pressures stressing you out. That includes having to drop off or pick up the kids, having to rush home to sort out tea or bath time, or having to contemplate sitting in traffic for an hour.

DEALING WITH STRESS

Stress is related very closely to change. When something in your life changes, even something relatively small can bring on symptoms of stress. Because our lives tend to be so hectic and constantly changing, feeling stressed can become the norm. This can lead to poor health and psychological problems. Starting up your own business is fraught with change and instability, so it is natural that when you are running your own company you will often experience the symptoms of stress, including feeling irritable, snappy, anxious or depressed, along with physical symptoms like headaches, migraines, indigestion and palpitations.

When this happens on a regular basis, or if you feel like it most of the time, you need to take some time out. We know this is easier said than done when you are juggling home and running a business, but both will suffer if you don't do it. As well as finding your personal wellbeing time during the day, schedule proper time out at weekends and holidays. Many owner/managers barely take holidays at all during the year, let alone the minimum four weeks that is the legal requirement for employees. You may think that working long hours and taking no holidays is just a temporary measure required to set your business up, but this is a fallacy. Businesses tend to be greedy things and will grow to absorb whatever time you allocate to them. As we mentioned earlier, there will always be something that needs to be done in your business and, if you let it, it will claim every waking (and a lot of sleeping) hours. The temptation is to say 'I'll sacrifice the next two years to the business so that it succeeds quicker and I can retire earlier. That way I can compensate for time missed with my family or friends later on when I'm rich'. In our opinion this is a mug's game. A lot can happen in the world of small businesses, and just because you dedicate 100 per cent of your time to it does not necessarily mean that it will be a success. Indeed, if you are constantly stressed, exhausted and guilty, you will not make good decisions and you won't be able to retain staff or think about the long term, both of which are key to business growth.

Surely the point of setting up your own business is that you are able to work on your own terms? This means that if you genuinely want to work on it 24/7 then you can. But in many cases, women decide to set up their own business precisely because it will enable them to work around their family or other commitments.

So take time out. Factor weekends and evenings and holidays into your calendar. Think about it – if you are functioning at a fraction of your capacity, then it is very likely that your business will be in a similar state.

LOOKING THE PART

As well as feeling well and balanced when you are running your own business, it is important to feel happy with the way that you look. If you are stressed, you are more likely to eat erratically, leading to weight loss or gain. Lack of sleep has an effect on your skin. Dehydration, caused by not drinking enough water and drinking too much coffee, tea or cola, will also make you look tired and worn out. Not having time to take stuff to the dry cleaners or buy new clothes means you find yourself wearing strange collections of things that you found at the bottom of your wardrobe. Working hard is often matched with playing hard, and late nights and too many vodka tonics will take their toll.

The key to feeling happy with how you look is to dress in the way you would like to be perceived by your customers. So if you want to be seen as professional and serious, wear suits. If you want to be seen as creative and individual, wear vintage. It is such a cliché, but first impressions really do count.

When we started out, because neither of us came from professional backgrounds and we were relatively young, we didn't have much of a clue about what image we wanted to portray to our clients. We were mostly working in the gap year industry which is pretty laid-back, but at the same time we still wanted to be taken seriously. The problem was that we found ourselves buying suits or jackets in black or grey because we thought that it was what professional people wore. We never felt really comfortable in suits though. Suits make you feel like you are at work, but they're a bit of a cop out in terms of making yourself stand out from the crowd as a distinctive individual with a distinctive business offering. What we needed was a radical make-over, and a way of looking like brilliant, successful, dynamic business people without wearing a boring suit.

The solution came about by accident, when we had a complementary session with an image consultant as part of an article we were writing. We had a colour-analysis session which involved us sitting in natural light with no make-up on, our hair scraped back and various scarves tied around our necks. The consultant showed us how some colours threw light back onto our faces, making us look slightly better (bearing in mind our adorned condition). Other colours drew colour from our faces and made us look a lot worse. Black, one of our staples for jackets and tops, made us instantly look terrible.

We also spent some time looking at body shapes and types, and how certain cuts of clothes suited each of us. What we came away from the session with was an understanding of what colours and shapes suited us. A key point was that while you do need to look like a professional person, you also need to stand out from the crowd. So while it is fine to wear suits, you need to make sure you customise them in such a way that they are personalised and that people remember you when they meet you. We then had to go away and rethink our entire wardrobes.

The outcome of this exercise was a total change in the way we dress for work. Now we each have a range of colours that we wear, and certain styles. This probably all sounds completely trivial, but it really does make a difference. Most people are very visual and will judge others instantly based on what they look like – either on a conscious or sub-conscious level.

We have gone on a massive learning curve in terms of the way we look over the last few years, and we both genuinely believe that if you are confident about your appearance, this will be conveyed to other people. We are definitely not fashion gurus and we still have our off-days, but these are some of the things which we have learned about looking the part when it comes to business:

★ Whenever possible, buy quality products. These aren't necessarily the most expensive things, but they are always better made and will last longer than your average bargain fashion purchase.

★ Work out what colours look best on you and stick to them. If you must wear black, keep it away from your face.

★ Be objective about your body shape and think about what proportions will work best for you.

★ Think about what aspects of your individual personality you most want to convey to others. Then find accessories, jewellery, scarves and secondary items of clothing (i.e. not jackets, trousers or skirts) that will help do this.

★ Think carefully about what signals the clothes you are wearing are sending out and how appropriate they are. Blinging accessories and fur ponchos might be appropriate for Victoria Beckham but, unless you are in the fashion industry, a footballer's wife or a pop star, you'll need to tone it down. Otherwise potential customers will be distracted by your clothes and won't remember what products or services you are offering. Make-up can also be distracting (think of any number of celebrities here), so if you do wear it (and most people do look better with some make-up on), keep it to a minimum.

★ It is often the details which let you down. The state of your hair, skin and nails can tell someone that you don't have time in the morning to get ready properly, that you are stressed, tired or downright careless. None of these things will work in your favour when talking to customers or clients.

By looking after yourself physically and mentally and keeping up appearances in terms of clothes and make-up, you will feel more confident about communicating with other people, especially strangers. This will make them listen to what you have to say, and remember you. When you are running your own business, you are your own best publicity, so make sure that you are projecting the right message.

TO SUM UP . . .

- ★ When running your own business it is vital to learn to manage your time.
- ★ Manage and set your own and other people's expectations of your time in advance.
- ★ Try to 'switch off' when you are not at work.
- ★ Talk to your partner and family about how running your own business may affect your time spent at home.
- ★ Don't try to do everything yourself – delegate at work and at home.
- ★ Be a bit selfish to preserve your sanity and health.
- ★ Learn to say 'No' to requests which can be done by someone else.
- ★ Decide on what is really important to your lifestyle and prioritise accordingly.
- ★ Take proper time out and do nothing.
- ★ Think about what clothes suit you and accessorise to make them individual.
- ★ Pay attention to detail when it comes to looking after yourself and your appearance.

8

Exit

EVEN when you are starting your business, you should have a picture in your mind of what direction you want the business to take, how long you want to run it for and how you plan to exit. It may be that you don't foresee the day when you will ever want out, and this is a perfectly valid goal to have. But usually you need to understand that when the day comes for you to step away from the business, you want to be able to sell it on (ideally) and cash in your chips. In order to do this, you need to have built the business in such a way that it does not depend upon you for its success. There are various ways you can do this, including creating capacity by building a strong team, or by setting the sales stream up in such a way that anyone can crank the handle and keep the products going out and the customer demand coming in.

Building something which is not reliant on you is more difficult when you are a 'one-woman band', whose business is built around your particular skills. At a certain level, if you are self-employed, then the business is you and your customers won't want an alternative. If this is the case, then resign yourself to the fact that – short of keeping it as a family business – the business won't outlive you.

When you are starting up, think carefully about the purpose of the business. Is it a means to an end, or is it an end in itself? If it is a means to an end, you will see it as an opportunity to make a large sum of money at some point in the future: you could consider selling it in a trade sale, taking it to a flotation or structuring it so that the management will buy it from you. If the business is an end in itself, you are doing it as a labour of love. Your primary motivation for setting it up is not to cash in your chips and make a packet at some future point, but to spend your time doing something that you love. When you stop wanting to do this, you could consider closing the business, handing it over to family to run or selling it outright. So you need to decide what you see your business being, how you see it growing in the future. If you don't see it growing at all and are quite happy working as a sole trader, that is fine, but be aware that you are unlikely to make a killing by selling it on one day. If you are a self-employed decorator, for example, you could well have a large list of customers and be making lots of money, but those customers won't necessarily want another decorator who they don't know taking over your business and being let loose in their homes. So be realistic about your goals and objectives.

HOW LONG DO YOU WANT TO RUN THE BUSINESS FOR?

This is an important question when it comes to planning your exit from the business. Do you plan on running your business for the rest of your life? Does it involve doing something which you love and which you can do up until, or even beyond, retirement age? If so, this is clearly a business which is an end in itself and the question of when to exit isn't relevant. However, there is the chance that you might get bored and want to change direction, in which case you should have a

Plan B (remember that?) which involves being able to shut the business down. If you are a sole trader and have no debts, this is a fairly straightforward process. If you do owe money and can't repay it, you could be made – or choose to be made – bankrupt, which obviously isn't straightforward. Always speak to an accountant or solicitor about your options before deciding to close a business down, or being forced to do so.

If you are a limited company, then closing your business is called 'winding it up'. It may seem rather odd, but it is vital that you think about what the natural conclusion of your business might be. If, for example, you decide to look for equity investment when you are setting up, then potential investors will want to know that you are committing for a good few years. Our business angels wanted to see a return after three years, so we knew we were committing ourselves to working in the company for at least that long. Venture capitalists will want to tie you in for a lot longer than that – or until the business is making enough money for them to realise their investment and get an optimum return. You need to be realistic about how long it might take to get your business up and running. Even if your business plan is saying that you will break even in the first year, make a profit in the second year and be ready to sell in the third year, be aware that there is a good chance that this won't happen. If this is the case, then how long are you prepared to stick around for? Before deciding on how you are going to exit from your business, you need to have an idea of how long you are going to run it for.

TO WHAT EXTENT DO YOU WANT OUT?

Wanting to sell your business outright is a very different scenario from wanting to get out of the management and day-to-day running of it. In many sale situations, the buyer will want you to stick around for a year or so to ensure a smooth hand-over of ownership. This would normally be a requirement in the buyer's terms and conditions, as long as you are bringing value to the business. If you don't want to sell outright, but want someone else to run it while you retain some shares, then there are various ways of doing this.

TYPICAL EXIT OPTIONS

There are a number of pathways which most owner/managers of businesses will consider as exit strategies. Below are the main routes to exit which you need to think about:

★ **selling to another business or individual**
★ **handing it on to your family**
★ **management buy out (MBO) or management buy in (MBI)**
★ **floating the business on the stock market**

The first option is one of the most obvious ways of parting with your business. Handing the business on to someone in your family is only going to be relevant for certain businesses and situations, and the same goes for company flotations. Management buy outs are when the management team purchases the shares in the company from the existing share-holders, and management buy ins are when a team of external people, usually funded by venture capitalists, buys the company shares. You may feel that none of these options is what you eventually want to do with your business, in which case there are other alternatives, such as merging with another business or winding the company up. You just need to think about what will suit your objectives best.

SELLING YOUR BUSINESS

Selling the business means getting everything shipshape in terms of your accounts, legals, intellectual property and admin. Any buyer will carry out due diligence on all these things, and not having them well organised could jeopardise a sale. The best way of sorting this out is by keeping on top of all your admin and legal requirements as time goes on. Keep everything filed and easily locatable.

You will also need to have a good team of staff to add real interest for a buyer. Sometimes in a trade sale a competitor will buy a business simply because the latter is occupying market space which it wants. In this case the buyer may cut loose any employees of the bought company and merge the business's other assets into its own. But usually a buyer will want to know you have a strong team in place, with a common vision of how the company can progress.

VALUING YOUR BUSINESS FOR SALE

Everyone has a different view of what a business is worth. An owner/manager often tends to have an inflated idea of their company's value, but it is a truism that a business is only worth what someone is prepared to pay for it. Different industries and sectors have different ways of valuing businesses, but expect that a potential buyer will be looking at your profits rather than your turnover. They will also want to see real evidence of growth and a future for the company. You need to believe that your valuation of the company's worth is based on market reality rather than your subjective opinion. You need to be able to prove that the business has lots of strengths apart from you, and that your customers will stick with it. A potential buyer will be reluctant to get involved with anything which is too reliant on the owner/manager for success.

Think of the tax implications

Selling shares in your business will be seen by the Inland Revenue as a capital gain, and you will be taxed accordingly. Always consult an accountant or tax specialist when you are making decisions about selling your business or selling shares. The last thing you want is to lose a large chunk of your hard-earned cash to the tax man at this stage.

KEEPING IT IN THE FAMILY

These days it is increasingly difficult to set up a business which you then pass on to your children to run. Young people nowadays have so many options when it comes to their careers that they are often reluctant to follow in their parents' footsteps. Of course, there are other family members who could take over the helm, but this can be fraught with difficulties and conflict. If this is an option that you want to consider, talk to your family as early on in the process as possible and sound out exactly what their views are. Don't assume that anyone else is going to jump at the chance to run your business.

MBOs AND MBIs

An MBO can be a good way of handing over your business into the hands of people who already know and are committed to it. If this is the exit route you wish to take, be clear about it as an objective and train your team to work together in such a way that you can step away and they can carry on seamlessly without you. They will need to raise cash to buy your shares, so you will need to give them notice of what your intention is and a chance to ask any questions. Be aware that during the honeymoon period, when employees first start working with a business, they are much more likely to be enthusiastic about owning a stake of it. As time goes on, they may well change their minds. An MBO isn't necessarily an all-or-nothing situation. The management team could buy chunks of the company as time goes on, depending on company performance and objectives being met. An MBO can be a positive way of selling your business, in that you know that you are handing it over to people who you have trained and who know the business. On the other hand, you need to build the team to make it happen and, as Chapter 3 has shown, this is no easy task.

MBIs are less common than MBOs, and there are many more risks involved which make them less likely to be successful. For some types of businesses, however (usually larger ones), they are an option.

FLOATING YOUR COMPANY ON THE STOCK MARKET

This is an ambitious target for any start-up. It can also be one of the most rewarding in terms of money and sense of achievement. However, this is not an appropriate goal for all businesses, and for many smaller businesses there would be no real advantage in being publicly listed. Nevertheless, it is a goal for many start-ups with high growth potential.

TO SUM UP . . .

★ Right from the start, think about how you want the business to end up.

★ Keep on top of all your legal, HR, administrative and other stuff which a buyer will want to look into.

★ Think about how long you want to run the business for.

★ Research the options for exiting your business and decide which is best for you, then write your business plan to fit into this goal.

The End?

THIS MAY BE THE END OF THE BOOK, but we hope it is the beginning of your business. Alternatively, if you are already running a business, we hope that this book has helped you to come to some informed conclusions about decisions that you need to make. With any luck we will have flagged up some of the pitfalls that start-ups can stumble into and you can now try to avoid these. Starting your own business is not an easy option when it comes to career choices. But along with the stresses and the problems comes a huge opportunity to set yourself on the steepest learning curve you are ever likely to encounter during your life.

What we have found is that, while you can prepare an end game for your business in the form of a three or even a five-year plan, there is no limit to the amount you learn and experience when you are setting something up yourself. Every challenge, every opportunity becomes the starting point for a new experience, which makes you more confident, more informed, a better thinker, communicator or empathiser. The better you are at making decisions, assessing risks and understanding others, the better your business will perform. As we have seen, simply by following the chapters in this book you will have to tackle creative thinking, researching, pulling numbers together, writing business and marketing plans and dealing with other people (some of whom you would never normally encounter in your daily life). You will also have to get used to problem-solving, spotting talent, organising yourself, being honest and open with your loved ones and balancing your home and your work.

The best thing about setting up and running your own business is that you are doing it on your own terms. You are doing it to improve the lifestyle of yourself and your family – financially, but in other ways too. Women in the 21st century are at the forefront of a massive change in the way that people choose to work. Most of us have to work, but we can choose the way in which we work. When you run your own business, you are able to choose your hours, to shift your priorities, to concentrate your efforts in a way in which you never normally can do when employed by someone else. In this sense, it is a hugely liberating experience. But with liberty comes responsibility, and you do need to consider carefully the fact that being your own boss means exactly that – and you will need to manage yourself and your business to get the most from the experience. When things go wrong, as they often will do, the responsibility will fall on your shoulders to sort it out. If the business is a roaring success but you have no work-life balance, then you will need to make some difficult decisions.

We face these kinds of decisions and responsibilities every day with our businesses. The amazing thing is that we have found we are capable of making those decisions. We are actually pretty good at what we do! And we could never go back to the 9–5 or having a boss again. Setting up our own business has changed our working lives for ever – it could do the same for you.

Useful Links and Numbers

Advertising Standards Authority
www.asa.org
Tel: 020 7580 5555

Alliance of Independent Retailers
www.indretailer.co.uk
Tel: 01905 612 733

Aurora: Advancing Women
www.auroravoice.com
Tel: 0845 260 7777

The Bag Lady: Global Directory of Women in Business
www.bagladyit.com
Tel: 0845 838 1451

British Chambers of Commerce
www.chamberonline.co.uk
Tel: 020 7654 5800

British Franchise Association
www.british-franchise.org
Tel: 01491 578050

Business Link
www.businesslink.gov.uk
Tel: 0845 600 9006

Business Network International
www.bni-europe.com/uk
Tel: 01923 891 999

Companies House
www.companieshouse.gov.uk
Tel: 0870 33 33 636

Copywriting and Writing Advice
www.ibruce.co.uk

Department of Trade and Industry
www.dti.gov.uk
Tel: 020 7215 5000

Direct Selling Association
www.dsa.org.uk
Tel: 020 7497 1234

Federation of Small Businesses
www.fsb.org.uk
Tel: 01253 336000

HM Revenue & Customs
www.hmrc.gov.uk
Tel: 0845 9154515 (for newly self-employed)

HM Treasury
www.hm-treasury.gov.uk
Tel: 020 7270 4558

Health & Safety Executive
www.hse.gov.uk
Tel: 0845 345 0055

Incorporated Society of British Advertisers
www.isba.org.uk
Tel: 0207 291 9020

Information Commissioner
www.informationcommissioner.gov.uk
Tel: 01625 545 745

Institute of Direct Marketing
www.theidm.com
Tel: 020 8977 5705

Market Research Society
www.marketresearch.org.uk
Tel: 020 7490 4911

National Federation of Enterprise Agencies
www.nfea.com
Tel: 01234 354055

National Readership Survey
www.nrs.co.uk
Tel: 020 7242 8111

The Prince's Trust
www.princes-trust.org.uk
Tel: 0800 842 842

Prowess: Promoting Women's Enterprise Support
www.prowess.org.uk
Tel: 01603 762 355

Small Business Service
www.sbs.gov.uk
Tel. 0845 001 0031

UK Business Directory
www.business-directory-uk.co.uk

The UK Patent Office
www.patent.gov.uk
Tel: 0845 9 500 505

INDEX